U0483678

符号中国 SIGNS OF CHINA

古 镇

ANCIENT TOWNS

"符号中国"编写组 ◎ 编著

中央民族大学出版社
China Minzu University Press

图书在版编目(CIP)数据

古镇：汉文、英文 /"符号中国"编写组编著. —北京：
中央民族大学出版社, 2024.3
（符号中国）
ISBN 978-7-5660-2321-6

Ⅰ.①古… Ⅱ.①符… Ⅲ.①乡镇—介绍—中国—汉、英 Ⅳ.①K928.5

中国国家版本馆CIP数据核字（2024）第016611号

符号中国：古镇 ANCIENT TOWNS

编　　著	"符号中国"编写组
策划编辑	沙　平
责任编辑	杨爱新
英文指导	李瑞清
英文编辑	邱　械
美术编辑	曹　娜　郑亚超　洪　涛
出版发行	中央民族大学出版社
	北京市海淀区中关村南大街27号　邮编：100081
	电话：（010）68472815（发行部）　传真：（010）68933757（发行部）
	（010）68932218（总编室）　　　（010）68932447（办公室）
经销者	全国各地新华书店
印刷厂	北京兴星伟业印刷有限公司
开　　本	787 mm×1092 mm　1/16　印张：11.875
字　　数	154千字
版　　次	2024年3月第1版　2024年3月第1次印刷
书　　号	ISBN 978-7-5660-2321-6
定　　价	58.00元

版权所有　侵权必究

"符号中国"丛书编委会

唐兰东　巴哈提　杨国华　孟靖朝　赵秀琴

本册编写者

康国剑

前言 Preface

古镇一般指有百年以上历史的、供人们集中居住的建筑群。中国有很多历史悠久、文化底蕴深厚的古镇，其中有上千年历史的古县就达800多个，古村镇5000多个，这在世界上是独一无二的。古镇是中华民族悠久历史的见证，是文化传承的重要载体，是宝贵的文化

Ancient town generally refers to a group of dwelling buildings with a history of over a hundred years. China is dotted with many ancient towns that enjoy long history and rich cultural heritage. Among these over 800 ancient counties and 5000 village towns boast more than a thousand years of history, and this is unique in the world. Witnessing the history of the Chinese nation and carrying cultural heritage, ancient towns are gems of culture, bringing up generations of honest, hardworking and intelligent people. Old houses in these towns are valuable and rare relics of ancient Chinese architecture.

遗产。古镇，养育了一代又一代淳朴、勤劳、智慧的人。古镇中的古民居是现今中国古代传统建筑稀有的遗存。

　　本书介绍了中国最具代表性的古镇，这些古镇至今仍有比较完整的古建民居，是不同地域、不同民族、不同建筑特色的中国古镇典范，展示了中国古镇丰富多样的风格和独特的魅力。

This book is intended to introduce the reader to some of the most characteristic ancient towns in China, where dwelling buildings are well preserved. These towns sit in different regions, are inhabited by different ethnic groups, and have different architectural features. With diverse styles and peculiar enchantment, they are the representative of all old towns of China.

目 录 Contents

中国古镇漫谈
Overview of Ancient Chinese Towns 001

古镇的选址与布局
The Location and Layout of Ancient Towns 002

古镇中常见的建筑类型
Common Building Types in Ancient Towns 004

古镇掠影
A Glance at Ancient Towns 019

江南古镇
Jiangnan Ancient Towns 020

华中古镇
Ancient Towns in Central China 064

东北古镇
Ancient Towns in Northeast China ················ 099

华北古镇
Ancient Towns in North China ······················ 107

西北古镇
Ancient Towns in Northwest China ··············· 126

华南古镇
Ancient Towns in South China ····················· 133

西南古镇
Ancient Towns in Southwest China ··············· 152

中国古镇漫谈
Overview of Ancient Chinese Towns

　　几千年的文化传承和历史流转，在中华大地上留下了无数各具特色的古镇。这些古镇最具生命力的特征，除了独特的建筑风貌、丰富的历史遗迹、古朴的环境氛围之外，还包括世代生活在古镇上的人。他们传统的生活方式、闲适的生活节奏、原汁原味的民风民俗，都是古镇风貌不可或缺的组成部分。

Thousands of years of history and civilization have given birth to countless ancient towns in the vast territory of China. These towns, unique in architectural style, rich in historical sites, and quaint in atmosphere, exude their distinctive flavor and delicacy. What is more, the residents who have lived there for generations are also an attraction. Their traditional way of life, the leisurely pace of life and the authentic folk customs are indispensable parts of the style and features of ancient towns.

> 古镇的选址与布局

中国古镇与古村落的选址和布局是十分讲究的。古人相信村镇与自然环境选定的成功与否，会直接关系到整个家族和子孙后代能否昌盛发达，所以在村镇建设之初，都要观察山脉的起伏、水流的方向、草木的生长等。

一般来说，村镇基地要选择地势宽敞平坦的地方，周围有山水环抱，最好是后有靠山、前有流水，周围有小丘护卫。江南和中南部的水乡古镇一般都建在河流的北岸，以取得良好的日照，一面临水或背山面水，建筑沿着河道伸展。临水设有码头，以联系水路交通。在东南和西南的山区，村镇往往是竖向分布的，形成层层交叠的布局。

> The Location and Layout of Ancient Towns

The ancients laid great emphasis on the location and layout of their towns and villages because they believed it would directly impact the prosperity of the whole family and future generations. As such, they would, before the construction of the villages, detect the ups and downs of mountains, the flowing direction of waters, the vegetation growth, and many more.

Generally, towns and villages would be built on a spacious and flat terrain, encircled by mountains and rivers. A place backed by mountains, fronted by river and flanked by small hills was what the ancients favored most. In regions south of the Yangtze River or South-central China, water towns are often located on the north bank of the river to get abundant sunshine; houses are

• 云南和顺古镇全貌
Full View of Heshun Town, Yunnan Province

在北方地区，村镇常选择地形平整的地方，整体布局严整而开阔，街道宽敞、建筑雄壮，凸显出北方大气、粗犷的风格。

built along the river, and the wharfs everywhere are the nexus of land and water transport. In mountainous areas of the southeast and southwest regions, towns and villages are usually built according to the hilly terrain at different levels, and they stand well-spaced. In the northern areas, towns and villages are generally found on flat terrain; their overall layout is thorough and open, and the spacious streets and magnificent buildings highlight an imposing and rough style.

> 古镇中常见的建筑类型

古镇中的建筑大致可以分为两大类，一类是住宅民居建筑，一类就是公共建筑（包括祠堂、寺庙、戏台、牌坊、街道等等）。这两类建筑通常都具有浓厚的地方特色和乡土气息。与大城市相比，各地的古镇更多地保留了明清以来的古代建筑，那些历经百年的古街、古桥、古宅院，带给人们的是一种古朴自然而又内涵深厚的文化意蕴。

民居建筑

民居就是人们居住的建筑，是最基本的建筑类型，分布最广，而且数量最多。各地古镇的民居不仅显现出多样化的面貌，而且保留了明清时期的建筑特色，记录了一个

> Common Building Types in Ancient Towns

Buildings in ancient towns can be roughly divided into two categories: residential houses and public buildings, the latter including ancestral halls, temples, opera stages, memorial archways, streets, etc. These buildings are usually imbued with strong local characteristics and flavors. Unlike big cities, these towns have more well-preserved ancient architectures of the Ming and Qing dynasties. The old streets, bridges and houses, with hundreds of years of history, brought to people a simple and profound connotation of natural and cultural implications.

Residential Houses

A residential house is a group of buildings where people live. It is the most common form of construction and

家族几代人的繁衍生息，见证了整个古镇的沧桑变化。

合院式民居

合院式民居是中国民居中十分常见的一种，以围合起来的院落为基本形式，而四合院是其中应用最广泛的一种。四合院大规模出现在元代时的北京等地区，到了明清时期，四合院成为中国民居中最为理想的一种模式，得到了长足的发展。

has the widest distribution and the largest quantity. Showing different features and appearances, these buildings retained the architectural features of the Ming and Qing dynasties, recorded how a family had lived and multiplied for several generations, and witnessed the changes in the whole town.

Residential House—Courtyard Style

The courtyard house, namely a courtyard surrounded by walls and buildings, is very common in Chinese residences. Among such houses, *Siheyuan* or Chinese quadrangles are the most common ones. In the Yuan Dynasty (1206-1368), *Siheyuan* came forth in large numbers in Beijing and some other areas; down

● **四合院示意图**

不同地区的四合院民居在房屋配置比例上有所不同，在四合院的基础上交错相连，组成院落和建筑群。

Schematic Diagram of *Siheyuan*

The location and quantity of rooms in *Siheyuan* vary according to different regions. However, no matter what changes are made, these courtyard houses or compounds are based on *Siheyuan*.

四合院，指的是东南西北四个朝向的房子围合起来形成的内院式住宅，其布局方式十分符合中国古代社会的宗法与礼教，家族中男女、长幼、尊卑地位有别，房间分配的区别也十分明显。而且其四周都是实墙，可以有效地隔绝外界干扰，且兼具防御功能，形成安全舒适的生活环境。四合院的形状、面积和单个建筑的形体只要略加调

to the Ming and Qing dynasties, it had developed by leaps and bounds, its architectural structure becoming the most perfect model of residential housing.

Siheyuan refers to houses with an inner courtyard surrounded by buildings from all four directions. Its layout is very much in line with traditional Chinese morality and Confucian ethics. In these compounds, different rooms are assigned to different family members—men and women, old and young, noble and

• 山西王家大院
晋中地区的宅院布局严谨，呈封闭结构，四周有高大围墙隔离，以四合院为建构组合单元，院院相连，沿中轴线左右展开，形成庞大的建筑群，以深邃富丽著称。

The Wang's Grand Courtyard, Shanxi Province
In central Shanxi Province, the courtyard has a rigorous structure, enclosed by high walls. Normally, these large compounds consist of several quadrangles, positioned successively along a central axis, looking magnificent and imposing.

整，就可以适应中国不同地区的地域条件，所以南北各地几乎都可以见到四合院的身影。其中最具代表性的就是北京四合院、晋中四合院、皖南天井院等。

- 皖南天井院

天井院即四周的房屋连在一起，中间围成一个小天井。由于皖南地区人口稠密，丘陵较多，建房屋时要尽可能节约用地，所以四面的房屋都建两层，围合成一个高而窄的天井，有利于采光和内外空气对流。

Patio in Southern Anhui Province

In such houses, buildings on all four sides are adjoined to form a small patio in the center. This area is densely populated and hilly, so people have to save as much space as possible in housing construction. The buildings often have two stories, and are enclosed to form high and narrow atriums, for easy lighting and ventilation.

humble-according to their age, gender or status. *Siheyuan* is always enclosed by solid walls, offering a comfortable, quiet and cordial space. The walls also provide security as well as protection. To adapt to many different geographical conditions in China, *Siheyuan* requires only minor adjustments to its shape, area and individual buildings. This is why it can be seen throughout China. Beijing *Siheyuan*, Courtyard in central Shanxi and Patio House in southern Anhui, among other courtyard houses, are the most representative ones.

- 古城丽江的汉风坊院

丽江的汉风坊院是汉族与白族建筑风格融合的产物，其基本模式是四合院，这类民居最有名的是"三坊一照壁"和"四合五天井"两种形式。

Han-style Courtyard in Lijiang

Based on *Siheyuan*, the Han-style courtyard is a fusion of Han and Bai architectural styles. The most fundamental forms of such houses are: (1) the principal room is built facing south and the yard is flanked by wing rooms; opposite the principal room is a screen wall; all these buildings are adjoined to form a courtyard; (2) four buildings reasonably surround five atriums in one courtyard.

窑洞民居

窑洞是中国西北黄土高原上古老的民居形式。黄土高原上的黄土层非常厚，不易倒塌，当地人利用高原有利的地形，凿洞而居，创造了窑洞建筑。窑洞一般有靠崖式窑洞、下沉式窑洞和独立式窑洞等形式。

在山西晋中地区的一些古镇

Cave Dwellings

Cave dwelling is a form of ancient residence found on Northwest China's Loess Plateau, where there is a thick layer of yellow earth, a type of soil that is solid and hard standing like walls. Taking advantage of this favorable condition, locals dug holes to create cave dwellings. Cliff-type caves, sunken caves and independent caves are common ones.

• 靠崖式窑洞示意图
A Schematic Diagram of Cliff-type Caves

中，保留着不少窑洞建筑。这些窑洞有的是在山崖和土坡的坡面上向内挖掘的靠崖式窑洞，还有一些富裕人家将窑洞与一般住宅相结合，后部是窑洞，前部留出空地建造平房，用院落围合，形成窑洞式的四合院。还有在平地向下挖掘一个方形大坑，再在四面坑壁上向内挖掘出下沉式窑洞，这也可以看作一种四面房屋的四合院。

干栏式民居

干栏式民居在中国西南地区分布较广，尤其是在苗族、侗族、傣族等少数民族聚居的地区。干栏式建筑盛行的地区，多为山峦起伏的

In some of the ancient towns in central Shanxi Province, there are many cave constructions. Some of these caves are built on a cliff face or an earth slope by digging inwards; in some cases, rich families combine caves with normal houses: constructing bungalows in open space in front of the caves, and then enclosing the courtyard with these bungalows to create a cave-style *Siheyuan*. Sunken caves are created by digging a large square pit in the ground; then on the four walls, caves are dug to create rooms; this can also be seen as a cave-like *Siheyuan*.

Pile-dwellings

Pile-dwellings are widely distributed

山区，而且气候潮湿炎热。当地人用当地生产的木材或竹子，随着地势建起两层的构架，下层一般多空敞而不做隔墙，里面用来饲养牲畜或堆放杂物。上层住人，而且四周向外伸出廊棚，主人可以在廊上起居休息。这种建筑的优点是可以通风防湿，又可防范山间野兽的侵袭。

土楼民居

在福建省南部永定、龙岩、漳州一带的乡村古镇，普遍存在一种土楼民居。每一栋土楼的体积

in Southwest China, especially in the areas inhabited by the Miao, Dong, Dai and other ethnic groups. These areas are mostly mountainous, with hot and humid climates. The Pile-dwellings, built according to the local terrain, are often two-storied and made of wood or bamboo. The lower floor is generally used as a livestock shed or utility room and has no walls; the upper floor is the living room and bedroom, its projecting parts serving as a corridor and canopy for resting and enjoying cool. These houses have the advantages of ventilation, moisture-proof, and wild animal defense.

- 下沉式窑洞
Sunken Caves

都很大，用夯土墙作为承重构件，平面形式有方形、圆形、五角形、八卦形、半月形等，以方楼和圆楼为主。土楼一般高三四层，其中房间多达数十间，可以容纳几十户人家、数百人生活。

古时福建地区战乱频繁，盗匪横行，于是人们建起高大坚固如堡垒般的土楼，整个家族的男女老幼都聚居在一起。土楼墙体厚重坚固，有的土楼甚至在三四层上开设枪眼，以抵御外敌。楼内还有谷

Tulou

Tulou can be found in the south Fujian regions of Yongding, Longyan and Zhangzhou. They are often huge, and the load-bearing walls are made of rammed earth. There are many types of earthen houses: square, round, pentagonal, octagonal, half moon, etc., square and round houses being the most common ones. Generally, *Tulou* has 3 to 4 stories and include dozens of rooms, enough to accommodate hundreds of people.

In ancient times, Fujian region was

● 湘西吊脚楼
Stilted Houses of West Hunan Province

仓、水井、牲畜棚圈等设施，如遇外敌围困可坚持数月之久。

公共建筑

古镇中的公共建筑种类十分丰富，常见的包括祠堂、寺庙、戏台、牌坊、桥梁等。

祠堂

祠堂是一个家族祭祀祖先的

plagued by wars and banditry, so people built many fortress-like houses for their families or communities. These houses are tall and sturdy, and some have gun ports on the third or fourth floor, in order to fend off outside attacks. Within the compounds, facilities such as barns, wells, livestock stalls can also be found, and resources are enough to last for several months even if the houses are besieged by the enemy.

- **福建初溪土楼群**

福建省永定县下洋镇初溪地区的土楼群由五座圆楼和数十座方楼组成，依山傍水，错落有致，与周围山坡上的层层梯田构成壮丽的景观。

Tulou Complex of Chuxi Village, Fujian Province

Consisting of five round buildings and dozens of square ones, the Tulou complex in Chuxi Village, Xiayang Town, Yongding County, Fujian Province sits at the foot of a hill and beside a stream. The well-arranged houses, set against the layers of terraced fields on the surrounding hillsides, looking majestic and magnificent.

地方。明代以前，只有帝王诸侯才能自设宗庙祭祀祖先，平民只能在家中祭祖。明代嘉靖年间，朝廷首次"许民间皆立宗立庙"。到了清代，民间祠堂大量出现，几乎各村各镇都有祠堂，其中还有宗祠、支祠和家祠之分。祠堂的功能除了祭祖之外，还是族长行使族权的地方，同时也可以作为家族的社交场所。一些地方的宗祠还附设学校，

Public Buildings

Public buildings in ancient towns are of wide varieties, including ancestral halls, temples, opera stages, memorial archways, bridges, etc.

Ancestral Halls

The ancestral hall (or temple) is where a family pays respect to their ancestors. Before the Ming Dynasty (1368-1644), only the emperors and dukes or princes

- 江西婺源江湾萧江宗祠
  Xiao ang Jiang's Ancestral Hall, Jiangwan Village, Wuyuan, Jiangxi Province

族人子弟就在这里上学。祠堂建筑一般都比民宅规模大，越有权势的家族祠堂往往越讲究，高大的厅堂、精致的雕饰，成为这个家族光宗耀祖的一种象征。

寺庙

中国古镇中还保留着大量的民间寺庙，除了具有宗教性质的佛教寺庵、道教宫观、清真寺之外，还有许多供奉传统和地方诸神仙的庙宇，如关帝庙、土地庙、文昌阁、魁星阁、真武阁等等。对于古代中国人来说，无论是传说中的文臣武将还是管天管地的各路神明，无论是外来的菩萨还是本土的神仙，只要能带来平安、圆满与护佑，就都可以纳入信仰和崇拜的范围，享受香火。

戏台

戏台常设于一村一镇最为繁华的地段，用于逢年过节戏班演戏或举行其他典礼仪式。这种戏台建筑一般独立高耸，一面或三面开敞，屋角向四面挑起，有飞扬般的轻盈感。戏台多雕梁画栋，风格华丽热闹。

had the privilege to set up their ancestral halls, and civilians could worship their ancestors at home. It was not until the Jiajing Period of the Ming Dynasty that the imperial court allowed civilians to set up ancestral halls or temples. In the Qing Dynasty (1616-1911), civil ancestral halls came forth in large numbers, with almost every village having its hall. These ancestral halls can be divided into three categories: ancestral halls, branch ancestral halls and family ancestral halls. In addition to worshiping, an ancestral hall is also reserved for the management and organization of clan affairs and social contact. In some ancestral halls there are schools where children of the clan attend. Normally, the ancestral hall is larger than a residential house in terms of size. Rich families usually have magnificent ancestral halls, a spacious hall with exquisite carving is a symbol of the wealth and power of a proud family.

Temples

In ancient Chinese towns, a great number of folk temples are preserved today. These temples include mosques, Buddhist and Taoist temples, and those dedicated to traditional and local deities, such as the Temple of Guan Yu (one

• 福建永定高陂关帝庙

关帝庙是为了供奉三国时期的蜀汉大将关羽而修建的，在全国各地都有。三国之后，历代帝王都曾对关羽加封号，后来关羽被推崇为"武圣"，与"文圣"孔子齐名。

The Temple of Guan Yu, Yongding County, Fujian Province

The Temple of Guan Yu is dedicated to Guan Yu, the famous general in the Three Kingdoms Period (220-280). The temples for Guan Yu are found everywhere around the country. Guan Yu was given various posthumous titles by emperors of past centuries, and addressed by people respectfully as the "Saint of War", a title that equals the "Saint Confucius".

牌坊

牌坊又称"牌楼"，是一种中国传统的门洞式纪念性建筑物，盛行于明清时期，在民间被广泛用于旌表功德、标榜荣耀。在古村

of the best-known Chinese historical figures), The Land Temple, The Temple of Wenchang (a Taoist dcity in Chinese mythology, known as the God of Culture and Literature), The Temple of Kuixing (a character in Chinese mythology, the God

- 云南剑川沙溪镇的古戏台

这座古戏台建于清光绪四年（1878年），第一层为戏台，其上为亭阁，整体木雕与建筑形式都具有鲜明的大理风格。古戏台是古镇的文艺活动中心，每到赶庙会的日子，人们就会在这里搭台唱戏，热闹一番。

Ancient Opera Stage in Shaxi Town, Jianchuan County, Yunnan Province

This opera stage was built in 1878. The ground floor serves as the stage while the upper floors are pavilions. Both the architecture and its wood carvings have distinctive Dali local style. The opera stage is the entertainment center of this town; during holidays, opera performances will be held here.

- 安徽省祁门县闪里镇坑口村会源堂古戏台

Ancient Opera Stage at Huiyuan Ancestral Hall, Qimen County, Anhui Province

镇中，牌坊一般安放在村口或镇中央，用来旌表和纪念某人某事，也可仅仅用来当做一种装饰。各地牌坊不仅建筑结构自成一格，而且通常集雕刻、绘画、匾联文辞和书法等多种艺术于一体，集中体现了古

of Examinations), The Temple of Great Emperor Zhenwu, etc. For the ancient Chinese people, the deities who can bring peace and luck will be worshiped, regardless of their origins.

Opera Stages

An opera stage, often standing in the busiest section of a town or village, is

• 安徽龙川"奕世尚书"坊

"奕世尚书"坊建于明嘉靖四十一年（1562年），为同属龙川胡氏家族的户部尚书胡富、兵部尚书胡宗宪所立。"奕世"，即"一代接一代"之意。

Yishi Shangshu Memorial Archway, Longchuan Village, Anhui Province

This archway was built in 1562 in honor of Hu Fu and Hu Zongxian, the two officials from one family. *Yishi* means "handing down from generation to generation".

人的生活理念、道德观和民风民俗，具有很高的审美价值和深刻的历史文化内涵。

used for opera shows or other ceremonies. The stage, with one or three sides open to the audience, is generally towering independently over other buildings. The upturned eaves of the construction deliver a sense of lightness, and the rich ornamentation is gorgeous and lively.

Memorial Archways

The memorial archway, also known as the decorated archway, is a kind of traditional doorway-type monumental building. It was popular in the Ming and Qing dynasties and was widely used by the ancient Chinese to praise virtues and achievements or demonstrate glory. These archways usually stand by the entrance or in the center of the towns. They are erected to praise or commemorate someone or something, or just for decoration purposes. Archways in different regions have their own distinctive styles, and always incorporate sculpture, painting, couplet, calligraphy and other art forms, embodying the ancient philosophy of life, morality and folk customs. They are of high aesthetic value and profound historical and cultural connotations.

古镇掠影
A Glance at Ancient Towns

　　历史悠久的古镇遍布中国各地，这些古镇中保存着大量古代建筑、历史遗迹，那些古意盎然的老街、店铺、祠堂、牌坊和民居，都带有鲜明的地方色彩和丰厚的文化内涵。

The historic towns can be found all over China. In these towns are a great many well-preserved ancient buildings, historical sites, quaint old streets, shops, ancestral halls, archways and houses, all with distinctive local flavor and rich cultural connotations.

> 江南古镇

　　江南地区的水乡古镇大多兴起于明清时期，古镇的建筑风格以朴素恬淡为主，既强调空间的开敞明晰，又有着浓郁的文化氛围。建筑一般依水势布局，色调以黑白的强

● 杭州西湖
West Lake, Hangzhou

> Jiangnan Ancient Towns

Most of the ancient water towns in Jiangnan region (regions south of the Yangtze River) were constructed in the Ming and Qing dynasties. Their architectural style is simple and tranquil, seeking a spacious and bright space

烈对比为特色，力图使整体居住环境达到完善优美的境界。水乡古镇虽然一般规模较小，但别具一番淳朴敦厚的乡土气息。

浙江古镇

浙江省气候温和湿润，自然风光秀美宜人，浙江古镇依山傍水，有着得天独厚的自然条件。古镇民居多建在山坡河畔，既适应复杂的自然地形，节约了耕地，又创造了

with a rich cultural atmosphere. The constructions, fitting in well with water, feature high-contrast black and white buildings, and everything looks perfect and harmonized. Though water towns are generally smaller, they enjoy a unique and unsophisticated rustic flavor.

Zhejiang Ancient Towns

Zhejiang is blessed with mild climate and beautiful sceneries. Owing much to these favorable conditions, ancient towns there are richly endowed by nature. The towns are mostly built according to the local terrain, saving land while creating a good living environment. To adapt to climate conditions and meet the needs of life and production, local people built courtyards, open-halls, atriums and passways in houses; from inside to outside they are

• 绍兴兰亭鹅池
Goose Pond of Lanting Garden, Shaoxing

良好的居住环境。根据气候特点和生产、生活的需要，建筑普遍采用合院、敞厅、天井、通廊等形式，使内外空间既有联系又有分隔，形成开敞通透的布局，给人一种朴素自然的感觉。

西塘

西塘位于浙江省嘉兴市嘉善县境内的江浙沪三省市交界处，古名"斜塘""平川"。相传在春秋时期，吴国大夫伍子胥大兴水利，

spacious, bright and well organized, designed simple and natural.

Xitang

Xitang, or "West Pond", formerly known as Xietang (Oblique Pond) or Pingchuan (Flat River), is situated in Jiashan County, Zhejiang Province at its border with Jiangsu Province and Shanghai Municipality. According to legend, in the Spring and Autumn Period (770 B.C.-476 B.C.), Wu Zixu, a famous Chinese scholar and military general, ordered to dig many canals and a pond to facilitate

● 西塘水乡风光
Scenery of Xitang

西塘河边的摇船
Awning Boats Docked on the Shore, Xitang

开凿了伍子塘，伍子塘之水直抵于此，故西塘亦称"胥塘"。西塘地势平坦，河流密布，自然环境十分幽静，镇里以"桥多、弄多、廊棚多"而著称，许多老街巷还保留着原有的风貌，十分淳朴。这个千年古镇保留着原汁原味的江南水乡风情和浓浓的生活气息。

在西塘古镇中最著名的要数那道长近千米、造型古朴的廊棚。所谓廊棚，就是指带屋顶的街。西塘

water transportation and to channel water to Jiashan County, and thus Xitang is also called Xutang (*Xu* Pond). Crisscrossed by rivers and streams, Xitang sits on a flat terrain, and is a very quiet place. The town houses many bridges, lanes and covered corridors, with many of the old streets and lanes retaining their original features. After a millennium, the authentic style of water towns in the region and rich flavor of life has not been washed away by the tides of history.

In Xitang, the most well-known

的廊棚并不都设在繁华地带，这里的廊棚有的临河，有的居中，有的在沿河一侧还设有一些靠背长凳，供人歇息。绝大多数的廊棚为砖木结构，浑然一色的墨瓦盖顶，沿河而建，连为一体，俗称"一落水"。

西塘古镇里有许多深宅大院，也就形成了长长的巷弄。现今镇上仍保留着122条长短不一的巷弄，其中有5条百米以上的宅弄，最有特色的一条

scene is the covered corridor which is nearly one thousand meters long and of simple appearance. It is actually a street with roof. Some sections of the covered corridors in Xitang are placed in the busiest section, while others are built along the river or the streets. Long chairs are arranged along the riverside of some covered corridors for people to have a rest. Most of them are built of bricks and wood and covered by black tiles. Linked together, they create a graceful posture.

The many large courtyard houses of Xitang form long lanes here. Today there are still 122 lanes of varying lengths in the town, among which five are over a hundred meters long. The most distinctive open-air lane is called "Stone Skin" lane. It got its name for the fact that it is flanked by two residential buildings.

● 水边廊棚
廊棚既可用来遮阳避雨，又可用来欣赏美景，游人漫步其中，思古之情油然而生。

Covered Corridor along the River
The covered corridor is used to keep off harsh sunshine and rain, and is also a good place to enjoy beautiful sceneries. Walking through it, visitors may muse over things of the remote past.

• 石皮弄
Stone Skin Lane

露天弄堂名叫"石皮弄"。石皮弄是夹在两幢住宅之间的露天弄堂，始建于明末清初。这条长弄全长68米，宽处1米，弄口最窄处仅有0.8米，路面由166块石板铺成，非常平整，下面为下水道。石皮弄左右两壁梯级状山墙有6—10米高，至今仍然保留完整。

醉园是西塘镇塔湾街的一处古民居，初建于明朝时期，整个庭院房屋至今保存完好。醉园共有五进院落，是一个老宅花园，园小而别

Built in the late Ming and early Qing dynasties, this lane is 68 meters in length and one meter in width, and the narrowest point at the entrance is only 0.8 meter wide. The path, paved with 166 stone slabs, is very smooth, underneath it being the sewage system. The walls on both sides of this lane are 6 to 10 meters high, and are still intact.

The Zuiyuan Garden is an ancient house in Tawan Street of Xitang, and its well-preserved buildings dated back to the Ming Dynasty (1368-1644). The garden, small and unique, includes a succession of five courtyards, in which delicate rockworks and winding aisles are ingeniously arranged. In the courtyard there is an exquisite tiny bridge made of bricks, which is ornamental and functional but allows only one person

西塘醉园
Zuiyuan Garden, Xitang

致，池石玲珑，回廊通幽。庭院里有一座仅容一人侧身而过的砖制袖珍小桥，看上去玲珑剔透，不仅具有观赏性，还具有实用性。在花园门对面朝南的墙上刻着"醉经堂"三个大字，"醉园"之名由此而来。醉经堂为清乾隆年间的著名书画家王志熙修建，园内至今还留有他的墨迹。

to pass through at a time. On the wall opposite the vase-shaped door are carved three characters "*Zui Jing Tang*" (The Hall of Intoxicating Books), from which the Zuiyuan Garden takes its name; the hall was built by Wang Zhixi, an eminent calligrapher and painter of the Qianlong Period of the Qing Dynasty, whose works can still be seen in this garden.

乌镇

乌镇位于浙江省桐乡市，这里地势平坦，河流纵横交织，气候温和湿润，物产丰富，素有"鱼米之乡、丝绸之府"之称，是典型的江南古镇。乌镇历史悠久，春秋时期，吴国曾在此屯兵，唐咸通十三年（872年）建镇。十字形的

Wuzhen

Wuzhen, a typical water town in Jiangnan region, is located in Tongxiang City, Zhejiang Province. The town lies on a flat terrain, and it is crisscrossed by rivers and streams. With mild climate and rich natural resources, it is reputed as "the Land of Plenty and the House of Silk". In the Spring and Autumn Period (770 B.C.-

- 乌镇风光 (图片提供：FOTOE)

乌镇堪称"百步一桥"，历史上桥梁最多时有120多座，现存30多座，最早的桥建于南宋，大多数桥重建于明清，有些桥还题有桥联，具有浓厚的历史文化气息。

Wuzhen Scenery

It is said that Wuzhen has a bridge every hundred paces. Historically there had been over 120 bridges, and about 30 survived till today. The oldest was built in the Southern Song Dynasty, and most were reconstructions in the Ming and Qing dynasties. Some bridges are inscribed with poetic couplets, exuding a strong historical and cultural atmosphere.

内河水系将全镇划分为东南西北四个区块，当地人分别称之为"东栅""南栅""西栅""北栅"。乌镇具有典型的江南水乡特征，至今仍完整地保存着晚清和民国时期水乡古镇的风貌和格局，以河成街，街桥相连，依河筑屋，水镇一体。

- 乌镇特产——蓝印花布

乌镇物产丰富，比如蓝印花布、丝绵、布鞋、木雕竹刻、乌锦、篦梳、湖笔、白水鱼、桐乡橘李、三白酒、姑嫂饼、杭白菊等。

Blue Printed Fabric as Wuzhen Specialty

Wuzhen boasts rich products, such as blue printed fabric, silk floss, cloth shoes, wood and bamboo carvings, brocade, combs, Chinese brushes, white fish, oranges and plums, *sanbai* liquor, *gusao* cake, chrysanthemum tea and others.

476 B.C.), the state of Wu had stationed its troops here, and in year 872, the town was established. The cross-shaped inland river systems divide the town into four sections, known locally as "East Quarter, South Quarter, West Quarter and North Quarter". Wuzhen has the typical features of Jiangnan water towns, its style and layout that took shape in the late Qing Dynasty and the Minguo Period (1912-1949) still remain untouched; waterways and roads interlock and are connected by bridges; houses are built along the river. The town and the rivers lie side by side, enhancing each other's beauty.

Similar to many other Jiangnan water towns, streets and residential buildings in Wuzhen are built along the river. What sets it apart from other towns is that some of the buildings have projecting parts over the river, supported by crossbeams resting on timber piles or stone pillars in the river bed. With planks spread out, these projecting parts serve as veranda, known as "Water Pavilion". These pavilions have windows on three sides, ideal for enjoying water scenery.

Situated in Guanqian Street of Wuzhen town, Xiuzhen Taoist Temple (The Temple of Taoist Cultivation) was built in 998. As a part of this complex, the

乌镇和许多江南水乡小镇一样，街道、民居都沿河而造。沿河的民居有一部分延伸至河面，下面用木桩或石柱打在河床中，上架横梁，搁上木板，人称"水阁"，这是乌镇特有的风貌。这种水阁三面有窗，凭窗可观沿河风光。

修真观是位于乌镇观前街的一处道观，始建于北宋咸平元年（998年），而修真观戏台是道

opera stage of Xiuzhen Temple was built in 1749. The stage, covering an area of 204 square meters, is a two-story building with hipped-gable roof and upturned eaves, appearing solemn and elegant; the wooden sparrow braces connecting the columns and beams are exquisitely carved, and of high artistic value; the ground floor, enclosed by brick walls, is fitted with two doors, the side one leading to the river pier; at the rear part is mounted a small staircase leading

- **修真观古戏台** (图片提供：FOTOE)

楼台分前后两部分，后部是化妆室，雕花矮窗，宽敞明亮；前部是戏台，正对广场。

Opera Stage, Xiuzhen Taoist Temple

This building is divided into two parts: the rear is a bright and spacious dressing room with carved lower windows; the front is the stage facing a square.

观的附属建筑，建于清乾隆十四年（1749年）。戏台占地204平方米，为歇山式屋顶，飞檐翘角，庄重中透着秀逸。梁柱之间的雀替均为精致的木雕，艺术价值极高。台为两层，底层用砖石围砌，进出有边门和前门。边门通河

to the stage. One can also board the boat directly from a special door in this building.

The bridges Tongji and Renji in Wuzhen East Quarter are collectively known as the "Bridge within a Bridge". Tongji Bridge, 28.4 meters long and 3.5 meters wide, is a one-curvature stone arch bridge and lies in an east-west direction,

- 晨雾中的"桥里桥"　（图片提供：FOTOE）
Bridge within a Bridge in Morning Mist

埠，底层后部有小梯通楼台，亦可通过翻板门从河埠下到船里。

乌镇西栅的通济桥和仁济桥合称"桥里桥"。通济桥是单孔石拱桥，长28.4米，宽3.5米，呈东西向。仁济桥长22.6米，宽2.8米，呈南北向，也是拱形结构。两桥直角相连，你中有我，我中有你，无论站在哪一座桥上，均可以欣赏到"桥里套桥"的景观。站在南河岸看过去，两桥的半圆形桥孔倒映水面，形成虚虚实实的圆环，十分漂亮。

while Renji is a south-north arch bridge with 22.6 meters in length and 2.8 meters in width. The two intersect at right angles, which looks harmonious and integrated. Standing on either bridge, you can enjoy the landscape of "Bridge within Bridge". Seen from south bank of the river, the semi-circular bridge openings with their reflections in the rippling water are very beautiful.

"元宵走桥"

乌镇有很多民间习俗，比如元宵走桥。农历正月十五为元宵节，俗称"正月半"，在乌镇有"走桥"的习俗。天黑下来后乌镇居民三五结伴出游，至少要走十座桥，路线不能重复，称"走十桥"。妇女们还会带上一只平时煎药的瓦罐结伴而行，过桥时将瓦罐丢入河中，寓意新的一年里无病无灾。

"Crossing Bridges on Lantern Festival"

Among the many folk customs in Wuzhen, crossing bridges on Lantern Festival is a real interesting one. Every 15th of the first month on the lunar calendar, when night falls, residents here would travel in the town, in groups of three and four, crossing at least 10 bridges, and would not walk the same route. When crossing the bridge, women would throw gallipots into the river to pray for health and good luck in the coming year.

南浔

南浔古镇位于浙江省湖州市东北，在江南古镇中建镇相对较晚，初建于南宋淳祐十二年（1252年），在明万历年间至清代中叶成为江南最富有的小镇。明万历年间，随着蚕丝业的兴起和商品经济的发展，南浔经济空前繁荣，至清代末年已成为全国蚕丝贸易的中心，民间有"湖州一个城，不及南

Nanxun

Established in 1252, the old town of Nanxun is located northeast of Huzhou City. Compared with other Jiangnan old towns, Nanxun is relatively young, but it was the richest one from the mid-Ming down to the mid-Qing dynasties. During this period, with the development of silk industry and rise of commodity economy, Nanxun experienced unprecedented prosperity, and developed into the center of China's silk trade at the beginning of 20th century. The town became the most prosperous one in Jiangnan region, producing hundreds of magnates. As a popular saying

- **南浔古镇通津桥** (图片提供：FOTOE)

通津桥位于南浔镇过去的中心地带，是十字形水系的交叉点。明清时期，通津桥畔是繁华的丝市。该桥最初建于宋代，清代曾多次重修，为单孔石拱桥，桥长28米，宽4米，拱高7.6米。

Tongjin Bridge, Nanxun

As the intersection of the cross river systems, Tongjin Bridge lies where used to be the center of Nanxun. It is a one-curvature stone arch bridge built in the Song Dynasty (960-1279) and renovated several times in the Qing Dynasty (1616-1911). The bridge is 28 meters long, 4 meters wide and 7.6 meters tall. In the Ming and Qing dynasties, a bustling silk fair was held near the bridge.

浔半个镇"之说，南浔由此一跃成为江浙雄镇，富豪达数百家。

南浔古镇环境秀美，历史上园林众多，自南宋至清代，镇上大小园林达27处，至今仍存的有嘉业堂藏书楼、刘氏小莲庄、陈氏颖园和张氏适园等。

百间楼位于南浔古镇的东北侧，相传是明代的礼部尚书董份为家中保姆、仆人居家而建，始

went, "What counts as a city in Huzhou is barely half the size of Nanxun."

The beautiful town of Nanxun once had a large number of gardens. From the Southern Song Dynasty (1127-1279) down to the Qing Dynasty (1616-1911) the town had housed as much as 27 gardens. Among the survived ones are the Jiaye Library, the Liu's Xiaolian Manor, the Chen's Garden and the zhang's Garden, etc.

• 南浔百间楼
Baijian Houses, Nanxun

建时约有百间楼房，故称"百间楼"。百间楼沿河蜿蜒而建，长约400米，又架长板石桥连接两岸。百间楼的山墙高低错落。沿河石砌护岸整齐，且有河埠，方便行人上岸、下船、搬运货物，又便于汲水。百间楼保持了明代建筑风格，白墙、青瓦、回廊、水埠、花墙、券门，具有浓郁的江南水乡风韵。

嘉业堂藏书楼与小莲庄隔溪相望，有小桥通连。此楼的创始人

The Baijian (meaning hundred) Houses sits in the northeast of Nanxun. Legend has it that it was built by a high official Dong Fen for his servants. It is said to have about one hundred buildings upon completion, hence its name. The 400-meter compound was built along the river. Nearby, bridges and wharfs are built to facilitate water and land transport. In Baijian Houses, one would see both the architectural style of the Ming Dynasty. The white walls with zigzagged tops, black tiles, corridors, ports, lattice walls,

嘉业堂藏书楼 (图片提供：FOTOE)
Jiaye Library

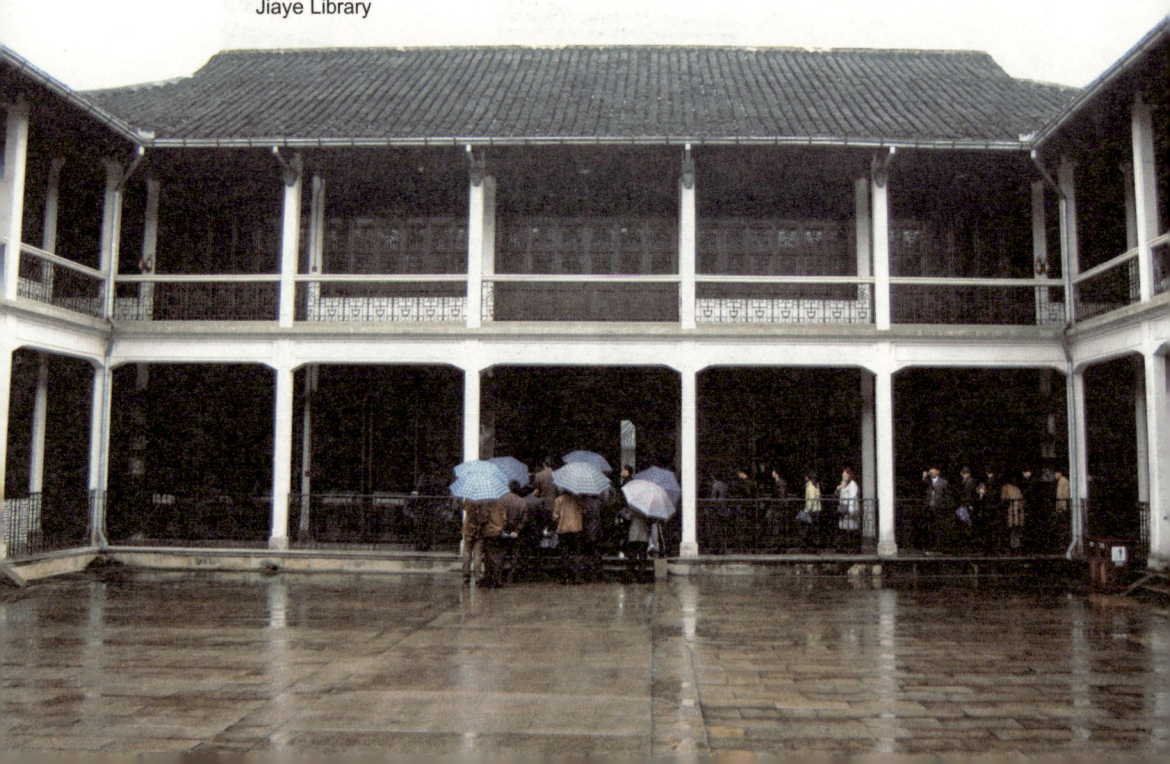

● 小莲庄荷花池 (图片提供：FOTOE)
Lotus Pond, Xiaolian Manor

是号称"江浙巨富"的晚清秀才刘承干。刘承干在清末曾捐巨资助修光绪帝陵墓，宣统帝曾赐以"钦若嘉业"的匾额，他以此为荣，故以"嘉业"为藏书楼命名。

嘉业堂藏书楼掩映在一座花园之中，为一座回廊式的两层建筑，共有书库52间，中间有大天井。在藏书楼全盛时期，即1925年至1932年间，楼中藏有各种珍本善

and round arched doors are all imbued with rich flavor of Jiangnan water towns.

The Jiaye Library stands opposite Xiaolian Manor across the river. The library was owned by Liu Chenggan, a mogul and scholar of the late Qing Dynasty. It took its name from a plaque inscription granted by Pu Yi.

Jiaye Library is a garden-like compound with winding corridors. The books are housed in 52 rooms of the two-

本书籍近万种，堪称中国历史上规模最宏大、藏书最丰富的私人藏书楼。

小莲庄又称"刘园"，位于镇南的鹧鸪溪畔，是晚清光禄大夫刘镛的私家花园及家庙所在。庄园始建于清光绪十一年（1885年），前后费时四十年，于1924年建成。因主人仰慕元代书画家赵孟頫所建莲花庄之名，取名"小莲庄"。小莲庄占地1.7万平方米，主要分外园和内园两部分，外园以荷池为中心，而内园的主体是太湖石堆砌的假山群。整个园林构思精妙，各处建筑分别成景，内园外园似隔非隔，错落有致，十分有趣。

江苏古镇

江苏省简称"苏"，位于中国东部沿海中心，地处美丽富饶的长江三角洲。江苏省地势低平，河湖众多，自然景观与人文景观交相辉映，有规模宏大的帝王陵寝、千年名刹，也有小桥流水的古镇水乡、精巧雅致的古典园林。江苏古镇大多地势平坦，水网密布，房屋多依水而建，民居自然融于

story buildings around a big atrium. In its heyday, between 1925 and 1932, the library kept thousands of rare books, and was considered the largest private library in Chinese history.

Xiaolian (Little Lotus) Manor, also known as the Liu Garden, sits by the Zhegu River in south of the town. It was built from 1885 to 1924 by local celebrity Liu Yong and his sons. The manor was so named for the fact that the Liu family was very fond of the Lotus Manor of the painter and calligrapher Zhao Mengfu of the Yuan Dynasty. Xiaolian Manor occupies an area of 17,000 square meters, and consists of inner and outer gardens. The outer garden is dominated by a lotus pond, while the main body of the inner one is a group of rockworks. The whole garden is ingeniously designed and arranged; halls, pavilions, corridors, towers are placed in a picturesque order, delivering an effect of a new sight at each step.

Jiangsu Ancient Towns

Also called "Su" for short, Jiangsu Province is situated on China's east coast, on the beautiful and fertile Yangtze River Delta, and well-known for its plain terrain and network of waterways. Jiangsu is represented by magnificent imperial

水、路、桥之中，青砖灰瓦、玲珑剔透的建筑风格，体现了江南地区纤巧、细腻、充满温情的水乡民居文化。

mausoleums, historical temples, water towns and classical gardens. Natural landscapes and man-made architecture coexist harmoniously. Most of the ancient towns in Jiangsu are densely covered by networks of waterways. Built along the river, the housing with grey bricks and tiles mixes well with waterways, roads and bridges. The dainty and exquisite architectural style shows the compact, delicate and warm residential culture of Jiangnan region.

- **太湖夕照**
  太湖位于江苏、浙江两省交界处，是中国的第二大淡水湖，属于大型浅水湖泊，湖区风景秀丽，有"太湖天下秀"之称。
  Sunset on Taihu Lake
  Taihu Lake is the second largest fresh water lake in China, on the border of Jiangsu and Zhejiang provinces. The lake is renowned for its beautiful scenery, and is hailed as "The scenery of Taihu ranks first in the world."

同里

　　同里镇位于江苏省吴江市的北部，建于宋代，至今已有一千多年的历史，是江南名副其实的水乡古镇。同里镇风景优美，镇外四面环水，为五个湖泊环抱，由网状河流将镇区分割成七个岛。

　　同里因水多，桥也多，镇内共有大小桥梁四十多座，大多建于

Tongli

The old town of Tongli sits in north of Wujiang City, Jiangsu Province. Built in the Song Dynasty (960-1279), it has over 1000 years of history and is a true water town of Jiangnan region. This picturesque town, embraced by five lakes, is divided by networked streams into seven isles.

　　Tongli features more than 40 bridges of varied sizes, most of which

• 同里风光
Scenery of Tongli

- **同里富观桥**

富观桥有一幅"桃花浪里鱼化龙"的石雕,传说一条鲤鱼想在三月春水暴涨的时候跃过龙门,脱去凡胎,化身为龙,可就在它跳出水面时,被过桥的一位漂亮姑娘吸引了,结果鱼头变成了龙头,身体却仍旧是鱼身。

Fuguan Bridge, Tongli

This bridge is adorned with a sculpture reflecting an old fable of how a carp had turned into a dragon. The story goes that a carp would like to take the opportunity of the spring floods in the lunar third month to jump over the dragon gate, so as to turn itself into a dragon. Just as it was jumping out of the water, it was attracted by a beautiful girl standing on the bridge. As a result, its head was transfigured into that of a dragon, but the body remained unchanged.

宋以后各时代。呈"品"字形架设在河道上的太平、吉利、长庆三座古桥,是昔日同里婚嫁花轿必经之桥,寓意吉庆。此外还有建于南宋宝祐年间(1253—1258)的思本桥,建于元至正十三年(1353年)的富观桥等。

同里的老房子多,大多建于明清时代,脊角高翘的房屋原貌,加

were built after the Song Dynasty. The three bridges of Tongli, namely Taiping (Peace), Jili (Good Luck) and Changqing (Long Felicity) are erected over the river in the shape of the Chinese character "品" (*Pin*). These bridges used to be the necessary passage where wedding sedan chairs went across as locals believed they would bring fortune and luck. Famous bridges in the town also include Siben

• 退思园闹红一舸

"闹红一舸"为一座船舫形的建筑，船身由湖石托起，外舱地坪紧贴水面。船头水中红鱼游动，点明"闹红"之意。

The Boat-shaped Building and the Goldfish, Tuisi Garden

In the shape of a boat, this building is supported by stones in the water. The front part of the boat is close to the surface of the water; goldfish swim around it, adding a lively sense to the whole building.

上走马楼、砖雕门楼、明瓦窗、过街楼等，充满了江南水乡古老小镇的文化韵味。

退思园建于清光绪十一年至十三年（1885—1887），园主名叫任兰生，落职回乡后花十万两银子建造宅园，取名"退思"，取史

Bridge built between 1253 and 1258 and Fuguan Bridge built in 1353, etc.

Tongli is home to a great many old houses dating from the Ming and Qing dynasties. These houses were built with flying eaves, brick-carved gate towers, translucent windows, and annexes such as arcade, exuding an antique and distinctive flavor of Jiangnan water towns.

Tuisi Garden or "Retreat and Reflection" Garden was built from 1885 to 1887 by a retired official Ren Lansheng at a cost of one hundred thousand taels of silver. Its name originated from an ancient dictum "Be loyal to the emperor when serving the court and reflect upon oneself when retreating from the post", which comes from a history book—*Zuo Qiuming's Commentary on the Spring and Autumn Annals*. Constructed according to local conditions, this compact garden enjoys elaborate design and unique layout. The most prominent part of the garden is a pool, surrounded by pavilion, terrace, porch and hall, which gives an illusion that these architectures are floating on the water, lending the garden a tranquil and elegant note.

Jiayin Hall was built in 1922. It was formerly known as "Liu's Mansion"

书《左传》中"进思尽忠，退思补过"之意。退思园的设计因地制宜，精巧构思，占地虽小，但布局独特。园以池为中心，亭台楼阁诸建筑如浮于水上，给人以清澈、幽静之感。

嘉荫堂建于1922年，房主名叫柳炳南，因此嘉荫堂旧称"柳宅"。嘉荫堂庭院高大宽敞，肃穆庄重。堂内各处建筑雕刻着许多精美的装饰图案，如架梁两侧中心刻有"八骏图"，梁两端刻有"凤穿牡丹"，梁底则刻有"称心如意""必定高中"等图文。更为罕见的是梁头上刻有取自中国古典小说《三国演义》的"古城会""三英战吕布"等八幅戏文的透雕，人物形象逼真，呼之欲出。

because its owner's name was Liu Bingnan. The high and spacious court is solemn and grand. The interior of the hall is adorned with various exquisite motifs; the two sides of the beams are carved with "Eight Horses", and the two ends are carved with "Phoenix and Peony"; the carvings "Satisfaction" and "Destined to Succeed" are found on the bottom of the beams; What's more rare is that the front beams are carved with eight pictures in *Romance of Three Kingdoms* including "Meeting in Ancient Town", "Three Warriors (Liu Bei, Guan Yu and Zhang Fei) Fighting against Lv Bu", etc. All the figures in these pictures are vividly portrayed.

• **嘉荫堂中精美的砖雕**
Delicate Brick Carvings of Jiayin Hall

• 嘉荫堂
Jiayin Hall

周庄

"烟雨江南，碧玉周庄"，始建于1086年的古镇周庄是一座典型的江南水乡小镇。周庄环境幽静，建筑古朴，至今仍保存着水乡集镇的风貌，全镇60%以上的民居仍为明清建筑。周庄还保存14座各具特色的古桥，形成一幅"小桥、流水、人家"的水乡风情画。

周庄的历史最早可以追溯到春秋时期，这里曾是吴王幼子摇的封地，称"摇城"。北宋元祐年间

Zhouzhuang

"Jiangnan is renowned for its fog and rain, while Zhouzhuang is well-known for its clear azure water." The old town of Zhouzhuang was built in 1086. A typical water town of Jiangnan region, it is endowed with tranquil environment and pristine architecture, and still maintains the style and feature of water villages. More than 60% of the residential buildings are Ming and Qing style architectures. Also, Zhouzhuang keeps 14 distinctive old bridges. All these create a

（1086—1094），官员周迪功将庄田200亩（13公顷）捐赠给全福寺作为庙产，当地人因此将这片田地称为"周庄"。元朝中叶，江南富豪沈佑、沈万三父子迁徙至周庄，因经商而逐步发迹，使周庄出现了繁荣景象。明清时期，周庄已经发展成为商业兴盛、人口稠密的江南大镇。

沈厅是周庄最大的民居建筑，原名敬业堂，清末改为松茂堂，由沈万三后裔沈本仁于清乾隆七年（1742年）建成。沈厅坐北朝南，共有大小房屋一百多间，占地两千多平方米。

scenery painting featuring small bridges, flowing water and elegant households.

The earliest record of Zhouzhuang can be traced back to the Spring and Autumn Period (770 B.C.-476 B.C.). What is today's town was then a prince's fiefdom known as "Yaocheng" (the Town of Prince Yao). After being donated to Quanfu (Full Fortune) Temple by Zhou Digong, in 1086 during the Northern Song Dynasty (960-1127), Zhouzhuang got its present name. In the mid-Yuan Dynasty, Shen You and his son Shen Wansan, the local merchants, moved here and rose to commercial prominence. Since that time Zhouzhuang started to boom. In the Ming and Qing dynasties, it developed into a large town with a flourishing business and dense population.

The Shen's Mansion, the largest residential building in Zhouzhuang, was formerly known as "Jingye Hall" and renamed "Songmao Hall" towards the end of the Qing Dynasty. It was constructed in 1742 by Shen Benren, Shen Wansan's

- 水乡古镇周庄
  Zhouzhuang

由三部分组成：前部是水墙门和河埠，供家人停靠船只、洗涤衣物；中部是墙门楼、茶厅、正厅，是接送宾客和议事的地方；后部是大堂楼、小堂楼和后厅屋，为生活起居之处。

位于周庄中心位置的世德桥和永安桥被称为"双桥"，均建于明代。因两桥相连，桥面一横一竖，桥洞一方一圆，样子像古代的钥匙，又称"钥匙桥"。如今，双桥已成为周庄的象征。

descendant. Facing south, the whole complex occupies an area of more than 2,000 square meters. Over 100 rooms are divided into three sections: the front part is the water gate and the wharf, where Shen's family moored boats and washed clothes; the middle part includes the gate tower, the tearoom and the main hall for serving guests and discussing business; the rear section is the living quarter consisting of several bedrooms.

The "Twin Bridges", which comprise of Shide Bridge and Yong'an Bridge, stand in the center of Zhouzhuang, and are considered the symbol of the town. Both were built in the Ming Dynasty (1368-1644). Shide Bridge is east-west and has a round arch, while Yong'an Bridge is north-south and has a square arch. Crossing the two crisscross rivers and connecting at the middle, the bridges look like an old-style Chinese key, also named as "Key Bridges".

• 沈厅松茂堂
Songmao Hall, Shen's Mansion

千灯

千灯古镇位于江苏省昆山市东南，毗邻闻名遐迩的周庄。一条清澈的小河穿镇而过，青瓦白墙的木结构民宅依河而建，四座清代石拱桥连通两岸。古镇原名"千墩"，相传是因吴淞江东北有墩九百九十九，与镇内一墩合成一千之数。清宣统二年（1910年），千墩更名"茜墩"，1966年易名"千灯"。

秦峰塔始名秦驻山塔，此地

Qiandeng

The old town of Qiandeng is located in the southeast of Kunshan City, Jiangsu Province, adjacent to the famous Zhouzhuang. A clear stream cuts through the town, where wooden buildings with white walls and black tiles were built along the water. Connecting the two banks are four stone arch bridges of the Qing Dynasty. Qiandeng (thousand lamps) was originally named "Qiandun" (thousand mounds), as the legend went that there were 999 mounds near the bank of Wusong River and one mound in the town. The town was renamed "Qiandeng" in 1966.

Qinfeng Pagoda, formerly known as Qinzhushan Pagoda, took its original name from a tall mound which once existed in this place. According to legend,

● 顾炎武像

千灯是明末清初杰出的思想家顾炎武（1613—1682）的故乡。顾炎武生于明末，他专心研习经世致用之学，写成《日知录》等著作近20种，被称为清初最有根底的学者。

A Portrait of Gu Yanwu

Qiandeng is the hometown of the outstanding thinker Gu Yanwu (1613-1682). As a scholar of the late Ming Dynasty, Gu was devoted to the application of classics. Among his many works are *Rizhi Lu* (Daily Accumulation of Knowledge) and others. Gu was deemed one of the most important scholars in the early Qing Dynasty.

原本有一个高耸的土墩，相传秦始皇统一中国之后，南下巡视，曾驻跸于此地，因而得名"秦驻山"。南北朝时期，佛教大兴，此地建寺修塔，始名"秦驻山塔"，后又改为"秦峰塔"。秦峰塔由塔基、塔身、塔刹三大部分组成，砖木结构，楼阁形式，平面呈方形，共有七级，高38.7米。塔的每只翼角上都挂有铜铃，风吹铃动，叮咚作响，声音可传到寺外。

after unifying China, the First Emperor of the Qin Dynasty made an inspection tour to the South and spent a few days here, hence the mound's name "Qinzhushan". In the Northern and Southern dynasties (420-589) when Buddhism prevailed, the pagoda was built here and got its name "Qinzhushan Pagoda", which was later renamed to "Qinfeng Pagoda". The seven-level, 38.7-meter pagoda is built of bricks and wood and square in section; it consists of three parts: foundation, body

- 千灯古镇
  The Old Town of Qiandeng

千灯古镇上的秦峰塔 (图片提供：FOTOE)
Qinfeng Pagoda, Qiandeng Town

and finial. At each corner of the eaves small wind bells are hung; the slightest breeze would swing the clapper and cause a melodious tinkling.

Mudu

Mudu, a historic town of Jiangnan region, is located next to Taihu Lake, 15 kilometers southwest of Suzhou. Surrounded by Lingyan and Taiping mountains, Mudu enjoys beautiful scenery and abundant natural resources. It also has over 2,000 years of history with its construction dating back to the Spring and Autumn Period (770 B.C.-476 B.C.). It is said that in this Period, Fuchai, the king of Wu, ordered to build a palace to please his beloved girl Xi Shi. She was tributed by Goujian, the King of the vanquished state, Yue. Then, numerous logs were carried here and they blocked the river. The Chinese character "渎 (*Du*)" means rivers and canals, so the town was named "Mudu" (river blocked by wood). Rivers and streams winding their ways through the peaceful town and the many old bridges and

木渎

木渎古镇位于苏州城西南15公里处，太湖之滨，是著名的江南古镇。古镇周边境内风光秀丽，物产丰饶，又恰在天平、灵岩等吴中名山环抱之中，所以被称为"聚宝盆"。木渎镇的初建可追溯到春秋时期，至今已有两千多年的历史。相传在春秋末年，吴越两国争霸，越国战败，越王勾践献美女西施于吴王。吴王夫差专宠西施，特地为

• 木渎古镇
The Old Town of Mudu

她在灵岩山顶建造馆娃宫，源源而来的木材堵塞了山下的河流港渎，"木塞于渎"，"木渎"之名由此而来。镇上河道纵横，古朴清幽，河上的众多古桥和绵延的石驳岸组成了美丽的水上风景。

木渎还有"园林之镇"的美誉，明清时镇上有私家园林二十多处，至今仍存有严家花园、榜眼府第、虹饮山房、古松园等多处古典园林。据说清代乾隆皇帝六次南

embankment stretching along the rivers form a charming water landscape.

Mudu, reputed as a garden town, had more than 20 private gardens during the Ming and Qing dynasties, among which the Yan's Garden, the Bangyan Mansion, the Hongyin Villa, and the Ancient Pine Garden are preserved till today. The town is so charming that Qianlong, the Emperor of Qing Dynasty, is said to have been here six times.

The Yan's Garden, situated in Shantang Street, Mudu town, was

巡，就有六次来到木渎，木渎古镇的魅力可见一斑。

严家花园位于木渎镇山塘街的王家桥畔，其前身是清乾隆年间苏州名士沈德潜的寓所。光绪二十八年（1902年），木渎首富严国馨买下此园后修葺一新，更名"羡园"。因园主姓严，当地人称"严家花园"。严家花园内的厅堂建筑宏敞精丽，进入后面的花园区域，建筑则变得精巧活泼，丰富多彩，楼阁、亭轩、廊榭错落有致，富于变化，体现出精湛的造园艺术。

originally the residence of the famous scholar Shen Deqian in Suzhou during the reign of Emperor Qianlong in the Qing Dynasty. In 1902, it was acquired by a local magnate Yan Guoxin who had it renovated and renamed it "Xianyuan Garden". As the owner was surnamed Yan, it was locally known as the "Yan's Garden". The halls in the compound are magnificent and elegant, while the garden in the rear section exhibits a sophisticated and lively quality. The richly varied pavilions, terraces, and open halls are cleverly arranged, reflecting exquisite skills of landscape architecture.

Hongyin Villa was the private garden of a scholar named Xu Shiyuan of the Qing Dynasty. Every time the Emperor Qianlong made his inspection tour to the South, he would visit this garden, so the locals called it the "Civil Summer Palace".

● **严家花园尚贤堂**
楠木大厅尚贤堂为明代建筑，体量宽敞，富丽堂皇，是主人接待贵宾、举行婚丧寿庆活动的重要场所。
Shangxian Hall (the Hall of the Virtuous), the Yan's Garden
Commodious and dignified, this phoebe-framed hall was built in the Ming Dynasty, and served for receiving distinguished guests and holding important ceremonies.

虹饮山房是清朝初年木渎文人徐士元的私家园林，乾隆皇帝南巡时每次经过木渎，必先在此弃舟登岸，入园游览。因而，当地人都把虹饮山房称为乾隆的"民间行宫"。

虹饮山房因靠近虹桥而得名，建筑风格融江南园林的秀美和北方皇家园林的壮丽为一体，由东西两处明代园林相连组成。东园原是明

Hongyin Villa takes its name from the Hongqiao Bridge nearby. Combining the exquisite elegance of southern landscaped gardens and the splendor and majesty of northern imperial compounds, it is made up of two small gardens of the Ming Dynasty. The eastern part used to be "Xiaoyin Garden" built by the Li family in the Ming Dynasty, known for its old trees, grotesque rocks and lush bamboo groves; the western part,

- 虹饮山房秀野竹堂
  Yezhu Hall (the Wild Bamboo Hall), Hongyin Villa

代李氏所建的小隐园，以老树、奇石和茂密的竹林著称。西园是秀野园，建成于明崇祯四年（1631年），以水景取胜，亭榭花木环池而构，参差错落，令人赏心悦目。

甪直

甪直镇位于江苏省苏州城东25公里处，古称"甫里"，又名"六直"。后因镇东有直港，通向六处，

constructed in 1631, is celebrated for the water features; the pool is surrounded by well-organized pavilions, terraces, flowers and plants, very pleasing to the eye.

Luzhi

The town of Luzhi, with the ancient name "Fuli", is located about 25 kilometers east of Suzhou. Once known as "Liuzhi", it took its present name from its water system that resembles the Chinese character " 甪 (*Lu*)". Luzhi boasts over 1,500 years of history and is praised as the "First Town of Chinese Watery Regions".

The town has 9 main streets, paved with pebbles and granite, and thickly lined with shops. Residential houses, either along rivers or streets, are mostly built in the Ming and Qing dynasties, with black tiles and white-washed walls, wooden doors and windows, and brick upturned ridges. Some of the walls are adorned with exquisite patterns. There are also 58 ancient lanes in the town, the longest being up to 150 meters.

◆ 甪直水乡风光
Scenery of Luzhi

甪直镇香花桥

香花桥建于清乾隆年间，是单孔花岗岩石拱桥，显得小巧玲珑。

Xianghua Bridge (the Bridge of Fragrant Flowers), Luzhi

Built in Qianlong Period of the Qing Dynasty, the bridge bears the name (Fragrant Flowers) and is a one-curvature arched bridge made of granite, small and exquisite.

水流形状很像"甪"字，故改名为"甪直"。甪直镇建于南朝梁天监二年（503年），迄今已有1500多年的历史，被誉为"神州水乡第一镇"。

甪直古镇上现有主街道9条，街面都以卵石及花岗石铺成，街坊临河而筑，前街后河，街道两旁店铺林立。不论临街的住宅还是临河的民房均为黛瓦粉墙、木门木窗、青

The town's most notable feature is its bridges, constructed in the Song (960-1279), Yuan (1206-1368), Ming (1368-1644) and Qing (1616-1911) dynasties. Owing to that, Luzhi deserves its reputation as a "Museum of Bridges". At one time, there were more than 70 bridges in this tiny town, 41 of which are preserved till today. The bridges are different in design and style, ranging from

砖翘脊，墙壁上还带有花纹，大多为明清时代的房子。镇中还有58条古巷，最深的巷子长达150米。

　　用甪直镇最大的特色就是水多、桥多，甪直也因此享有江南"桥都"的美称。在一平方公里的古镇区内原有宋、元、明、清时代的石拱桥70多座，现存41座，造型各异，各具特色，古色古香。甪直的石桥包括多孔的大石桥、独孔的小石桥、宽敞的拱形桥、狭窄的平顶

the multi-arch stone bridge, the single arch small stone bridge, the spacious arched bridge to the narrow flat-topped bridge, as well as two bridges intersecting at right angles and parallel bridges, etc., all of which show an antique flavor.

Founded in 503 of the Southern Dynasty, Baosheng Temple is dubbed "one of the top 4 temples of Jiangnan Region". Luzhi owed much of its rise and prosperity to the establishment of this temple—the temple flourished to promote

● 甪直古街巷
Ancient Lane, Luzhi

桥，也有两桥相连成直角的双桥以及左右相邻的姊妹桥和方便镇民的平桥。

保圣寺建于南朝梁天监二年（503年），是一座著名的千年古刹，被誉为江南四大寺院之一。用直镇的兴起与保圣寺的建造与繁盛有着密切的关系，可以说用直的繁

the prosperity of the town. Xiao Yan, an emperor of the Southern dynasties, went in for large-scale construction of temples. Baosheng Temple is the architecture from that period. In its heyday, the temple had more than 5,000 halls and rooms as well as thousands of monks, and its area covers half the town. Today, the 9 clay statues of arhats created by a famous

• 保圣寺
Baosheng Temple

• 沈宅乐善堂
Leshan Hall, Shen's Mansion

sculptor named Yang Huizhi of the Tang Dynasty are well preserved after a thousand years.

The Shen's Mansion, located east of Baosheng Temple and built in 1870, is the former residence of Shen Bohan, an educator of Luzhi. The Shen family used to be millionaires whose wealth was said able to buy half of the town. The compound of architectural style of the Qing Dynasty has a delicate layout; the pillars and beams are adorned with lavish carvings and paintings. Leshan hall, the main hall in this compound, is the essential part of the Shen's mansion and the most luxurious building in the town. Lavished with exquisite carvings, it is tall and spacious, warm in winter and cool in summer.

Shanghai Ancient Towns

Shanghai, situated on the Yangtze Estuary, is one of the largest cities of China and the world. With a history

华是"以庙兴镇"。梁武帝萧衍笃信佛教，大兴寺庙，保圣寺即当年建造的大寺之一。最盛时保圣寺有殿宇5000多间，僧众近千人，范围覆盖半个用直镇。如今，保圣寺保存着唐代著名雕塑家杨惠之所塑的9尊泥塑罗汉，虽历经千年沧桑，仍然完好。

沈宅位于保圣寺以东，建于清同治九年（1870年），是用直教育家沈柏寒的故居。建筑布局精巧，画栋雕梁，具有清代建筑特点。沈家原为甪直富豪，拥有众多的产业，当时有"沈半镇"之称。正厅乐善堂是沈宅的精华部分，也是镇上最豪华的建筑，高大宽敞，雕饰遍布，冬暖夏凉，四季皆宜。

spanning over two thousand years, Shanghai was originally a small fishing village. In the Spring and Autumn Period (770 B.C.-476 B.C.), it used to be in the territory of Wu, where in the Warring States Period (475B.C.-221 B.C.) a city was established. "Shencheng" was the oldest city in Shanghai region; after repeated relocations, it was settled near Sheshan Mountain in the Three Kingdoms Period (220-280) and got its

- **上海城隍庙**

  城隍是道教传说中守护城池的神明，上海地区供奉城隍由来已久，早在宋淳祐七年（1247年），华亭即立城隍庙。上海老城隍庙坐落在上海市内最为繁华的地区，始建于明永乐年间（1403-1424），距今已有近600年的历史。

  City God Temple, Shanghai
  One of the Taoist gods, the City God is the guardian of a city. In Shanghai area temples were dedicated to the City God long times ago, as early as in 1247, a City God temple was established in Huating. The Old City God Temple of Shanghai, located in the busiest region, was constructed between 1403 and 1424.

上海古镇

上海，地处长江入海口，是中国第一大城市，也是世界大都市之一。上海古时为海边渔村，已有两千多年历史。春秋时，上海地区属于吴国，战国时开始建城。"申城"是上海地区最早的城市，后来城址几经变迁。三国时期，申城城址于佘山附近固定下来，更名为name "Huating". In the Tang Dynasty (618-907) Huating county seat was established here while Shanghai town in the north of the county was gradually developed.

Zhujiajiao

Zhujiajiao, also known as "Jiaoli", sits in Qingpu district, Shanghai. This old town enjoys favorable location, and is crisscrossed by watercourses, along

朱家角河上的乌篷船 (图片提供：FOTOE)
A Black Awning Boat on the River of Zhujiajiao

"华亭",唐朝设县,华亭县北部的上海镇也逐渐发展起来。

朱家角

朱家角又称"角里",位于上海市青浦区中南部,地理位置十分优越。镇内河港纵横,9条长街沿河而伸,千栋明清建筑依水而立,36座石桥古风犹存,名胜古迹比比皆是。早在宋元时期,朱家角地区已形成集市,因水运方便,商业日渐繁盛,至明万历年间已经成为繁荣的大镇,是周围百里乡村的农副产品集散地。

古镇上的深宅大院很多,均为明清建筑,历史上许多富贵人家和文人雅士在此建园造宅,全镇古宅建筑有四五百处之多。作为水乡古镇,朱家角水多、桥多、河埠多,造型各异的石桥、千姿百态的缆船石布满全镇的大河小巷。

放生桥是江南地区现存最大的五孔大石桥,全长70.8米,宽5.8米,结构精巧,形态美观。明隆庆五年(1571),慈门寺僧人性潮募款建造此桥。桥的设计采用超薄的桥墩,加上桥拱自然递增,全桥形

which stretch nine long streets. In the town historical sites abound: hundreds of ancient dwellings built during the Ming and Qing dynasties stand by the river, and the 36 stone bridges, spanning in different shapes and styles, exude an air of antiquity. As early as the Song and Yuan dynasties, country fair was formed in Zhujiajiao region and the commerce had further flourished due to the convenient water transport. By the Wanli Period of the Ming Dynasty, the region has become a large and prosperous town as well as the distribution center of rural agricultural and sideline products from the countryside around.

The old town houses a great deal of imposing dwellings of Ming and Qing dynasties. Historically many wealthy people and literati built houses and gardens here, thus giving rise to the four or five hundred ancient dwellings in the town. As a water region, Zhujiajiao is represented by waterways, bridges and wharfs. Bridges and mooring stones of different shapes and styles can be found in every river and lane of the town.

Fangsheng Bridge (Set Free Bridge) is a five-arch stone bridge. 70.8 meters long and 5.8 meters wide, it is the largest of its kind in Jiangnan region. This bridge

● 放生桥（图片提供：FOTOE）
Fangsheng Bridge

成一个缓和的纵坡，自然衔接两岸街面，显得雄伟而不笨重。桥上的石刻也十分精彩。明清时，每月农历初一，当地僧人都要在桥上放生活鱼，故名"放生桥"。

圆津禅院始建于元至正年间（1341—1368），是朱家角著名的佛教禅宗寺院，因院内供奉观音菩萨，又名"娘娘庙"。禅院北临漕港，东傍珠溪，院舍结构小巧，殿内佛像不多，但都精雕细刻，庄严肃穆。清代初年，圆津禅院的第

of compact design and beautiful shape was built in 1571 with funds collected by a monk from Cimen Temple. The bridge has a gentle slope as it adopts ultra-thin piers and arches with modest size changes, spanning naturally across the river, which looks majestic but not bulky. The stone carvings on the bridge are also exquisite. In the Ming and Qing dynasties, on first day of lunar months, local monks would release live fish into the river on the bridge, hence its name.

Built during 1341-1368, Yuanjin Temple is a well-known temple in

● 圆津禅院 (图片提供：FOTOE)
Yuanjin Temple

三代住持语石大师擅长绘画和金石之学，之后的几任住持也都能诗善画，因此常有文人雅士在此聚会吟诗，酬唱往还。清顺治十五年（1658年），寺院进行了大规模修葺，增建了不少建筑，其中以清华阁最负盛名，这里不仅是名人文士珍藏书画之处，而且环境优美，登上清华阁远眺，朱家角的胜景尽收眼底。

金泽镇

金泽镇位于上海市青浦区的西

Zhujiajiao. It is also named the "Temple of Goddess" for the fact that it enshrines the statue of Avalokitesvara (*Guanyin*). The temple sits by two rivers; its premises are small, and the few statues of Buddha are carved with great skills, creating a stately and solemn presence. In the early Qing Dynasty, the 3rd-generation abbot of this temple and a few of his successors were specialized in either painting, epigraphy or poetry, so literati and scholars often held poetry saloons and literary discussions here. In 1658, it experienced major repairs, with many new constructions added,

南，是上海唯一与江苏省和浙江省交界的镇，水陆交通便捷，是江浙沪的重要交通枢纽。金泽镇历史悠久，人文景观众多。据史料记载，金泽原有"六观、一塔、十三坊、四十二虹桥"，全镇现存古桥21座，是上海保留古桥最多的镇，所以有"江南第一桥乡"之称。尤其在下塘街一带，一段350米的河道上并列的五座古桥，跨越了宋、元、明、清四个朝代，所以有"四朝古

including the most prestigious Qinghua Pavilion. Overlooking from this beautiful pavilion where paintings and calligraphic works are kept, one would have a scenic panoramic view of Zhujiajiao.

Jinze

The town of Jinze, sitting southwest of Shanghai's Qingpu district, is the only town that borders the two provinces, Jiangsu and Zhejiang. With convenient land and water transport, it is an important transport hub linking Shanghai, Jiangsu

● 金泽古镇 (图片提供：FOTOE)
The Old Town of Jinze

桥一线牵"的说法。其中的普济桥是上海地区最古老的石拱桥。

　　普济桥在金泽镇南首，因桥畔有圣堂庙，故俗称"圣堂桥"。此桥建于南宋咸淳三年（1267年），明清两代都曾重修，为单孔石拱桥，桥长26.7米，桥高5米，与万安桥非常相似，故合称为"姐妹桥"。普济桥所用的石料是珍贵的紫石，有紫色的光彩。每当雨过天晴，阳光照射在桥上，紫石晶莹的光泽，绚丽多彩。

and Zhejiang. Jinze has a long history and a good many of cultural landscapes. According to historical records, there had been "Six temples, a tower, thirteen archways, forty-two bridges" in Jinze, among which 21 old bridges survive till today. It is the only town that has so many old bridges in Shanghai region, thus earning itself the accolade "the Top Bridge Town of Jiangnan Region". The five bridges spanning parallel over the 350-meter river course in the vicinity of Xiatang Street in particular, were built respectively in the Song, Yuan, Ming and Qing dynasties, so there was a saying "Bridges of four dynasties are stringed by one river." Of the five, Puji Bridge, built in 1267, is the oldest stone arch bridge in Shanghai region.

　　Located south of Jinze, Puji Bridge is next to Shengtang Temple, and is commonly known as "Shengtang Bridge". It was built in the Southern Song Dynasty (1127-1279) and renovated in the Ming and Qing dynasties. With one arch, the bridge is 26.7 meters in length and 5 meters in height, very similar to the Wan'an Bridge, therefore the two being collectively known as the "Sister Bridges". Puji Bridge is built of a very precious purple stone—fluorite. Washed

● 普济桥 (图片提供：FOTOE)
Puji Bridge

● 万安桥 (图片提供：FOTOE)
Wan'an Bridge

万安桥位于金泽镇北，桥名取自"万世安祥、万民安业"。桥长29米，宽2.6米，是金泽最大的石桥，有"金泽四十二虹，万安桥居首"之称。此桥建于宋代景定年间（1260—1264），历经800多年，依然庄严雄伟。万安桥为弧形单孔石拱桥，坡度平缓，跨度大，结构坚固，形态优美。

by rain, the bridge appears shiny purple under the sun, sparkling and colorful.

Wan'an Bridge lies north of Jinze and takes its name from a dictum "Peace and serene for thousands of generations, good and prosperous life for all people". The 29-meter long and 2.6-meter wide stone bridge is the largest in the town, and is dubbed "Of the 42 bridges, Wan'an is the top one." Built in the Jinding Period of Song Dynasty, it still looks majestic and vital after 800 years of wearing-out. Wan'an Bridge is of single-arch type, with gentle slope, large suspension, solid structure and elegant shape.

> 华中古镇

华中地区包括安徽、江西、湖南、湖北等省，以徽派古镇和湘西古镇最为著名。徽派古镇的特点是建筑比较密集，屋顶坡度陡峻，翼角高翘，装修精致富丽，雕刻彩绘很多，总体风格秀丽轻巧。而湘西古镇多为汉族与少数民族杂居地区，无论是建筑风格还是民风民俗都带有浓郁的多民族特色。

安徽古镇

安徽省是中国古镇、古村落最为集中的地区，在古徽州府所辖的南部山区，众多古民居村落展现出鲜明的地域文化特色。徽州民居

> Ancient Towns in Central China

Central China includes Anhui, Jiangxi, Hunan, Hubei and other provinces, and the ancient towns of this area are represented by those of Huizhou and Xiangxi styles. In Huizhou-style ancient towns, buildings are usually crowded together. The buildings feature upswept eaves, roofs with very steep slope, delicate and ornate decoration, lavish carvings and paintings, the overall architectural style being beautiful and exquisite. However, Xiangxi region is inhabited by Han and ethnic groups, and the architectural style as well as the folk customs comes with strong multi-ethnic traits.

Anhui Ancient Towns

Anhui has the highest concentration of ancient villages and towns in China. In

- 白墙黛瓦的徽州民居
Huizhou Residential Buildings with White Walls and Black Tiles

从整体布局到建筑风格无不具有浓郁、独特的文化特征和古朴的生活气息。徽州古村落建筑中的民居、牌坊、祠堂并称为"徽州三绝",细节精致,清丽高雅,充分体现了古徽州的富庶和雅致。

the mountainous area of its southern part which was under the jurisdiction of ancient Huizhou Prefecture, a good many of old villages and dwellings show a distinct geographical and cultural feature. From the overall layout to the architectural style, Huizhou vernacular

• 徽州民居门窗上的精美木雕

旧时，徽州木雕多用来装饰建筑物或家庭用具，根据实际需要，采用圆雕、浮雕、透雕等手法，华丽繁复，极富装饰性。

Exquisite Wood Carvings on Windows and Doors of Residential Buildings, Anhui Province

In olden times Huizhou wood carvings were mostly used to decorate buildings and household appliances. According to actual needs, different techniques such as shallow relief, round carving and fretwork would be adopted. Gorgeous and complex, the carvings are highly decorative.

西递

西递坐落于安徽省黄山南麓，由于河水向西流经这里，原称"西

architectures are rich and unique in cultural traits and exude an antique flavor of life. Residential buildings, memorial archways and ancestral halls are regarded as the "three wonders of Huizhou ancient architecture". The superior workmanship and refinement of these buildings fully reflect the affluence and elegance of the ancient Huizhou.

Xidi

Xidi, formerly known as Xichuan (westward stream) because of the streams that run westward through it, is located at the southern foot of Huangshan Mountain. It used to be a postal service station in old times, hence the name Xidi (westward delivery).

Built during the Huangyou Period of the Northern Song Dynasty, the village has long been inhabited by people of the same clan—the Hu family. The prosperity of Xidi peaked in the 18th and 19th centuries, at which time the village comprised about 600 gorgeous houses. Xidi is a treasure house of ancient residential buildings, among which 124 simple and elegant residences from the Ming and Qing dynasties are well preserved. In the town, Hui-style buildings are artistically arranged; the

川";又因古有递送邮件的驿站，故而得名"西递"。

西递村始建于北宋皇祐年间（1049—1054），是一处以宗族血缘关系为纽带，胡氏家族聚族而居形成的古村落，至今已有960多年历史。18世纪到19世纪，西递的繁荣达到顶峰，当时村里有大约600座华丽的住宅。西递是古民居建筑的艺术宝库，至今尚保存古朴典雅的明

streets and lanes are all paved with stone slabs and the old buildings are usually of wooden structure complete with brick walls; exquisite wood, stone and brick carvings can be seen everywhere as decorations. The overall layout of lanes, streams and buildings is natural and reasonable.

Hu Wenguang's Memorial Archway, formerly Xidi Archway, lies at the entrance to Xidi Village. It was built

- 西递民居
  Buildings in Xidi

西递凌云阁
Lingyun Hall, Xidi

in 1578 at the behest of the emperor in recognition of Hu's achievement in his post. Unlike other archways around Huizhou, this archway, 12.3 meters high and 9.95 meters wide, is 5-storied, with exquisite stone carvings and a magnificent structure. On the flower board of the main plaque are carved various animal patterns such as deer, crane, tiger, leopard; on both sides of the board are coiling dragons by way of relief, under which is carved with figures—civil and military officials, symbolic of bringing peace and stability to the country.

Located to the west of Hu Wenguang's Archway, Lingyun Hall was built during the Daoguang Period of the Qing Dynasty,

清民居124幢。徽派建筑错落有致，所有街巷均以青石铺地，古建筑为木结构、砖墙维护，木雕、石雕、砖雕丰富多彩，巷道、溪流、建筑布局相宜。

　　西递村口的胡文光刺史坊俗称"西递牌楼"，明万历六年（1578年），皇帝批准在此建造这座功德牌坊，以表彰从西递村走出的官员胡文光在任期间的功绩。胡文光刺史坊与徽州各地的牌坊式样不同，有5个层次分明的楼阁，称为"楼阁式"。它高12.3米，宽9.95米，石雕古朴精湛，造型富丽堂皇。正楼

● **西递村口的胡文光刺史坊**
Hu Wenguang's Memorial Archway, Xidi

的匾额上雕有鹿、鹤、虎、豹等图案，两旁盘有浮雕的双龙，双龙图下是文官和武将，喻意安邦定国。

凌云阁位于胡文光牌坊西侧，俗称"走马楼"，始建于清代道光年间（1821-1850），相传是当年西递的首富胡贯三为迎接亲家、当朝宰相曹振镛的到来而突击营造的。凌云阁共分上下两层，粉墙墨瓦，飞檐翘角。在凌云阁下有单孔石拱桥，名为"梧赓古桥"。西溪流水环绕凌云阁，穿桥而过。

胡氏宗祠是胡氏家族祭祀列祖列宗之所，同时兼作宗族议事、婚嫁喜庆以及训斥不肖子孙的地方，是西递村中最大的祠堂。胡氏宗祠始建于明代万历年间，后毁于战火，清乾隆年间重建后，面积近2000平方米，整个西递都是以它为中心而布局的。祠堂整体建筑风格粗犷古朴、庄严肃穆，内部空间广阔，气势宏伟。

棠樾

棠樾位于歙县城西6公里处，以东西走向长达千米的石板路为主街，向南向北又有众多小街，古

commonly known as "Zouma Hall". This building is said to have been constructed by a wealthy person Hu Guansan to receive his noble relatives, the prime minister of the period, Cao Zhenyong. It is a two—story building with white painted walls, black tiles and upswept eaves. Next to Lingyun Hall is a single-arch stone bridge, Wugeng Old Bridge, spanning over a river that runs around the hall.

The Hu Ancestral Hall is where Hu family worships their ancestors; it is also reserved for clan discussions, wedding ceremonies, and rebuking unworthy descendants. Constructed in the Wanli Period of Ming Dynasty and later destroyed in a war, this ancestral hall was rebuilt in the Qianlong Period of the Qing Dynasty. It covers an area of nearly 2,000 square meters, the largest in Xidi. The design and layout of the entire Xidi village is based on it. This ancestral hall features a style of rugged simplicity and exhibits a solemn and stately bearing; the interior space is so vast that it looks magnificent.

Tangyue

Tangyue, located 6 kilometers west of Shexian county seat, is dominated by an east-west stone road of about a thousand

● 胡氏宗祠
Hu Ancestral Hall

祠、古亭、古牌坊、古民居星罗棋布，点缀其间。明清两代，棠樾徽商崛起，人文荟萃，出了很多名儒显宦。他们在家乡祭祖先、建祠堂、修牌坊，在棠樾形成了独具特色的牌坊群，棠樾因此被誉为"牌坊之乡"。

meters long, which is joined by many narrow alleyways running in a south-north direction. These alleys are dotted with a legion of ancient ancestral halls, pavilions, archways and residences. In the Ming and Qing dynasties, Huizhou merchants from Tangyue achieved commercial success, and many of them

棠樾共有七座牌坊，连成一线，以"忠、孝、节、义"石牌坊为核心，由两边向中间依次排列，呈半弧形展开。棠樾牌坊令世人惊叹的不仅在于它精美的石雕艺术，还在于建筑风格的独特及构造的巧妙。这些石头牌坊在建筑时不用上钉或铆，也没有用钢筋水泥来连接，只是将石头与石头巧妙衔合而屹立百年不倒。

became business tycoons or officials. On returning home they built mansions, ancestral halls and archways to honor their ancestors, giving rise to the group of distinctive memorial archways in Tangyue, which was hailed as "The Town of Archways".

In Tangyue there are seven memorial archways standing along a curving road with the four—"Loyalty, Filial Piety, Chastity and Charity"—as the key

- 棠樾古牌坊群
Ancient Memorial Archways in Tangyue

- #### "乐善好施"坊

"乐善好施"坊建于清嘉庆二十五年（1820年）。据说当时棠樾鲍氏家族已有"忠""孝""节"牌坊，独缺"义"字坊。掌握江南盐业命脉的盐官司鲍漱芳捐粮十万担，捐银三万两，修筑河堤八百里，发放三省军饷，于是，朝廷恩准在棠樾村头建"乐善好施"的义字牌坊。

Charity Memorial Archway

This archway was built in 1820. It is said that the Bao family of Tangyue was short of a "Charity" archway to make a whole set of "Loyalty, Filial Piety, Chastity and Charity". Bao Shufang, a member of the Bao family and also a high-ranking salt official of Jiangnan region, donated a large sum of money to the imperial court and built riverbanks, so the family was finally authorized by the court to build the "Charity" archway.

祠堂，是古代中国人祭祀祖宗或先贤的庙堂。棠樾的牌坊群旁有两座祠堂，一为鲍氏敦本堂，俗称"男祠"；一为鲍氏妣祠，又名清懿堂，俗称"女祠"。

敦本堂又称"鲍氏支祠"，坐北朝南，整个祠堂的结构简洁明

archways. What makes people marvel at these archways is not only their exquisite stone carvings but also the unique architectural style and ingenious design. Neither nail and rivets nor steel and concrete can be seen on these buildings. Cleverly joined, rocks and stones alone made them stand over a hundred years.

鲍氏支祠敦本堂
Dunben Hall—the Bao Branch Ancestral Hall

了，银杏为柱，樟木作梁，砖、木、石雕丰富而洗练不繁，处处透露出儒家的人生理念和文化内涵，显示出不偏不倚的"中和"之美。

清懿堂是全国唯一的女祠，又称"鲍氏妣祠"，建造于清嘉庆初年。祠堂作为封建宗法制度的产物，一向是男人们决议族中大事、惩罚违背族规者和供奉祖宗牌位祭

The ancestral hall is where the ancient Chinese people pay respects to their ancestors. Next to the memorial archways stand two ancestral halls: the Dunben Hall for men and the Qingyi Hall for women, both were built by the Bao family.

Dunben Hall, also known as the "Bao Branch Ancestral Hall", was built facing south. The hall is succinctly structured,

祀的地方。在男尊女卑的时代，女性均与祠堂无缘，名字不能列入宗谱，女性祖先在祠堂里也没有牌位。清懿堂打破先例，专为女性而建，女性不但可以入祠祭祀，共商女性大事，堂内还立有女性祖先的牌位。祠堂坐南朝北，结构紧凑，造型流畅，端庄而不刻板。尤其是

• 敦本堂内宋代理学家朱熹手书的"廉节"二字

"*Lian Jie*" (Honesty and Integrity) in Handwriting of Zhu Xi, the Famous Philosopher of the Song Dynasty, Dunben Hall

constructed of ginkgo-wood columns and camphorwood beams, decorated with exquisite but not redundant bricks, wood and stone carvings. The whole compound is permeated with Confucian philosophy of life and cultural connotation, presenting to the eye an impartial beauty.

Qingyi Hall is China's only ancestral hall reserved for women. It is also known as "The Ancestral Hall for Bao's Deceased Mother", built around 1800. In olden times, the ancestral hall, established under the feudal-patriarchal system, was reserved for clan discussions, worshiping the ancestors and punishing violations, and was used only by men. Due to the inferior social status of women, no ancestral hall was dedicated to them; their names were not allowed to place in the genealogy and there was no memorial tablet for female ancestors in the ancestral hall. However, Qingyi Hall set a precedent by setting up a place exclusive for women to pay respects to ancestors and discuss women's affairs, and the hall also enshrines female ancestral tablets. Facing south, the hall is of compact and smooth design, dignified but not rigid. In particular, the walls shaped like the character "八" (eight) outside the hallway are lavished with exquisite brick

• 清懿堂
Qingyi Hall

门厅外的八字墙，满饰砖雕，玲珑剔透，被誉为古徽州祠堂砖雕之最。

棠樾鲍家花园原为清代乾隆、嘉庆年间著名徽商鲍启运的私家花园。花园以徽派盆景为主题，同时荟萃了国内各流派盆景的代表作品，是一处品位较高的盆景观赏基

carvings, which are regarded as the finest brick carvings in Huizhou ancestral halls.

The Bao's Garden was formerly the private garden of a famous merchant, Bao Qiyun of the Qing Dynasty. Covering an area of 24 hectares, themed on the Hui-style bonsai, this garden has a rich collection of distinguished bonsai works of various schools. The bonsai on display

地。该园占地约24公顷，园内盆景品类齐全，形式多样，玲珑活泼，意趣横生。

take diverse forms and present exquisite and lively appearances, full of novelty and charm.

● 鲍家花园
The Bao's Garden

江西古镇

　　江西省地理位置独特，赣北与安徽接壤，所以这里的古镇民居多为徽派建筑。赣中地区古镇民居属于典型的赣式建筑。而赣南地区由于与福建相邻，古镇建筑则以客家民居为代表。

Jiangxi Ancient Towns

Jiangxi Province enjoys a unique geographical position. Its neighbors are Anhui Province in the north and Fujian Province in the south. In the northern part, residential buildings of ancient towns are mostly of Huizhou style; in the central area, old towns are dominated by typical Jiangxi-style houses, and in southern part of the province Hakka residences are the representatives.

• 庐山风光

庐山地处江西省北部，以雄、奇、险、秀闻名于世，素有"奇秀甲天下"之誉。

Scenery of Lushan Mountain

Lushan Mountain, located in the northern part of Jiangxi Province, is noted for its sheer peaks and precipices, varying clouds and fogs, silver springs and flying waterfalls. It is often hailed as "The unique and beautiful scenery of Lushan Mountain rank first in the world".

江湾

江湾古镇位于江西省婺源县城东20公里处，地处一片三山环抱的河谷地带。江湾始建于隋末唐初，最初有人家在江湾河湾处聚居，始称"云湾"，北宋时改称"江湾"。自唐以来，江湾便是婺源通往皖、浙、赣三省的交通要塞，为

Jiangwan

The old town of Jiangwan sits 20 kilometers east of Wuyuan County, Jiangxi Province, in a river valley surrounded by mountains on three sides. The town was established in the late Sui and early Tang dynasties. It was originally named "Yunwan" when someone first came here to live by the bend of the river,

- **婺源风光**

婺源县位于江西省东北部，是徽州文化的发祥地之一。这里山明水秀，自古文风鼎盛，素有"书乡"和"茶乡"之称，被誉为"镶嵌在赣、浙、皖三省交界处的绿色明珠"。

Scenery of Wuyuan

Wuyuan County, situated in the northeastern Jiangxi Province, is one of the birthplaces of Huizhou culture. With picturesque mountains and streams, plus strong literary atmosphere since ancient times, Wuyuan earns itself the accolade "Land of Culture" and "Hometown of Tea" as well as "The green pearl set where Jiangxi, Zhejiang and Anhui provinces meet".

婺源东大门。这里山水环绕、风光旖旎、文风鼎盛。

　　萧江宗祠又名"永思祠",始建于明朝万历六年(1578年),以其建筑规模宏大、雕刻精美、建筑材料考究而著称。据史料记载,北宋神宗元丰二年(1079年),萧氏一族为避难迁到云湾,改为江姓,"萧江"子孙逐渐繁衍成云湾的大族,于是把地名改成"江湾"。作为婺源最大的宗祠,萧江宗祠占地面积达2400平方米,是一组坐北朝

and renamed "Jiangwan" in the Northern Song Dynasty (960-1127). As the east gate of Wuyuan, Jiangwan has been the transportation hub linking Wuyuan and the three provinces—Anhui, Zhejiang and Jiangxi—since the Tang Dynasty. Encircled by mountains and rivers, this area boasts picturesque landscapes and strong literary atmosphere.

　　Constructed in 1578, and Jiang's Ancestral Hall or Yongsi Ancestral Hall is known for its grand scale buildings as well as exquisite carvings and top

• 江湾镇的徽派建筑
Huizhou-style Architecture, Jiangwan

南的徽派建筑，分前院、前堂、中堂、后堂四进。前院为宽敞花园，设有半月形莲花池。前堂、中堂和后堂的建筑巧饰雕琢，各具特色。

培心堂是江湾镇一栋清代徽商建筑，具有徽州民居的典型特征，共有三进，前进店面，中间住宅，后进厨房。培心堂门楣上写着"乐山安宅"四个字，取自孔子"仁者

• 萧江宗祠永思堂内景
Interior of Yongsi Hall, Xiao and Jiang's Ancestral Temple

grade building materials. According to historical records, in 1079 a clan surnamed "Xiao" took refuge in Yunwan and changed their surname to "Jiang". Later, their descendants became the most prosperous clan here, so the place was renamed "Jiangwan". Built facing south, the Xiao and Jiang's Ancestral Hall occupies an area of 2,400 square meters, the largest of its kind in Wuyuan. It includes a succession of four sections front courtyard, front hall, middle hall and rear hall. The front courtyard is a spacious garden, with a half-moon lotus pond; the buildings in the front, middle and rear halls are skillfully decorated with carvings, each with its own feature.

Peixin Hall is a compound built by Huizhou merchants of the Qing Dynasty. The compound is of typical Huizhou-style and has a succession of three sections; the front section is served as a shop, the middle as living quarters and the rear as a kitchen. On the lintel of Peixin Hall are inscribed four characters "*Leshan Anzhai*" (Benevolence makes the family happy and stable), taken from the saying "The wise find joy in water; the benevolent find joy in mountains" presented by Confucius. This is the moral idea that Huizhou merchants followed

乐山，智者乐水"，体现了徽商的经商和道德理念。穿过门厅，是一个正方形的小院，小院南墙下是一道端庄秀雅的砖雕石库门楼，各种花卉、人物、鸟兽的砖雕吉祥图案栩栩如生。正厅宽阔高大，前有天井，东墙开有花窗，上方悬挂"培心堂"匾，置身其中，令人倍感幽静典雅。

in doing business and life. On entering through the hallway, one is greeted by a small square courtyard, on south wall of which is built a stone-framed gate tower with a variety of lively brick carvings such as flowers, figures, birds and animals. The main hall, tall and spacious, faces an atrium and has a lattice window on its east wall; above this window hangs a plaque bearing three characters "*Pei Xin Tang*" (Peixin Hall). In this hall, one would find tranquility and elegance.

- 江湾镇古戏台
  Ancient Opera Stage, Jiangwan

婺源的油菜花

婺源被誉为中国最美丽的乡村之一，而婺源一年中最美季节就是三月中下旬油菜花开时节。每当春暖花开，漫山遍野的油菜花从山顶铺散到山谷，站在山顶望去，大片的油菜花层层叠叠，一望无际，中间围拢着几个小小的村落，黑瓦白墙的徽派民居点缀在一片金黄之中，构成一幅天人合一的画卷。

Cole Flowers in Wuyuan

Wuyuan is known as one of the most beautiful countrysides in China, while the most beautiful time of Wuyuan is the middle to the end of March when the cole flowers are in full bloom. In the warm Spring, a sea of cole flowers covers every hill and valley. Overlooking from top of the hill, one can see cole flowers, tier upon tier, stretch as far as the eye can see, with several small villages dotted about. Houses with white-painted walls and black tiles mix with the golden flowers to create harmony between man and nature.

- 婺源长滩的油菜花
  Cole Flowers in Changtan, Wuyuan

景德镇

景德镇坐落在江西省东北部,素有"江南雄镇"之称。镇上制瓷历史悠久,瓷器质地精良,是中外著名的瓷都。景德镇从汉代开始烧制陶器,东晋始制瓷器,距今已有1600多年的历史。景德镇瓷器造型优美、品种繁多、装饰丰富、风格独特,以"白如玉,明如镜,薄如纸,声如磬"的独特风格蜚声海内外。青花瓷、玲珑瓷、粉彩瓷、颜色釉瓷合称景德镇四大传统名瓷。

Jingdezhen

Jingdezhen sits in the northeast of Jiangxi Province, and has always been hailed as the "Key Town of Jiangnan Region". It is known as the "City of Porcelain" because it has been producing quality pottery for 1,600 years. Jingdezhen's porcelain boasts beautiful appearances, rich varieties, colorful decorations and unique styles. It has become known internationally for being "as white as jade, as bright as a mirror, as thin as paper, and as sound as a bell". Blue and White porcelain, Rice-pattern Decorated porcelain, Famille Rose porcelain, Color-glazed porcelain are collectively referred to as Jingdezhen's four traditional porcelains. Eggshell porcelain wares are regarded as magical treasures, while statuary porcelain is Chinese traditional artwork.

- **景德镇窑青白釉凸雕花卉纹鬲鼎式炉(南宋)**
  青白釉是一种釉色介于青白之间的瓷器,在北宋(960—1127)时期由景德镇工匠在白瓷的基础上创烧,最大的特点是胎质细洁、釉色青莹、色质如玉。

  Bluish-white Glazed Incense Burner with Floral Pattern Carved in Relief (Southern Song Dynasty 1127-1279)
  The bluish-white glazed porcelain, with a color between blue and white, was created in Jingdezhen in the Northern Song Dynasty (960-1127). Based on white porcelain, its most notable feature is the fine and clean porcelain body, the crystal blue glaze and the jade-like color.

薄胎瓷被人称为神奇珍品，雕塑瓷为中国传统工艺美术品。

景德镇御窑遗址博物馆位于原御窑厂遗址内。御窑厂是明清时期专为宫廷生产御用瓷器的，始建于1369年。它是我国历史上烧造时间最长、规模最大、工艺最为精湛的官办瓷厂，如今海内外拍卖价格最高的瓷器大多出于此。

The Jingdezhen Imperial Porcelain Museum is located on the site of the original imperial kilns. The imperial porcelain factory was set up in 1369 to produce porcelain exclusively for the imperial court of the Ming and Qing dynasties. In Chinese history, it was the government—run porcelain factory with the longest production history, the largest scale and the most exquisite craftsmanship, the porcelains auctioned off at highest prices at home and abroad being mostly produced in this factory now.

• 景德镇古窑遗址
The Site of Ancient Kilns in Jingdezhen

● 瑶里镇古建筑群 (图片提供：FOTOE)
Ancient Buildings, Yaoli

　　瑶里镇可以说是景德镇瓷业的发源地，景德镇瓷器的主要原料——高岭土就产于瑶里附近的高岭山。瑶里古名"窑里"，正是因瓷而得名，远在唐代中叶，这里就有生产陶瓷的手工业作坊。

　　The old town of Yaoli is the birth place of Jingdezhen porcelains, and kaolinite clay—the chief raw material is produced in Kaolin Mountain in the vicinity of this town. Yaoli, where the ceramic-making workshops appeared as early as the mid-Tang Dynasty, took its name from porcelain.

景德镇四大名瓷

青花瓷、玲珑瓷、粉彩瓷、颜色釉瓷，合称景德镇四大传统名瓷。

青花瓷创烧于元代，是以色料在坯胎上描绘纹样，施釉后经1300℃左右的高温烧成，釉色晶莹、雅致，透着一种素净、低调的古韵。

玲珑瓷初创于明宣德年间，是瓷工用刀片在坯胎上镂成点点米粒状，再填入玲珑釉料，入窑烧制而成。在清代，瓷工把青花和玲珑瓷巧妙地结合成一体，形成了青花玲珑瓷。玲珑瓷往往和青花相配，透明的玲珑和幽静的青花互为衬托，显得清新古朴。

粉彩瓷也叫"软彩瓷"，创烧于清代康熙晚期。因调淡雅柔和，有粉润之美，故被称为"粉彩"。粉彩颜色柔和，画工细腻工整，有国画韵味，体现浓郁的民族特色。

颜色釉瓷被誉为"人造宝石"，制作工艺是在釉料里加上某种氧化金属，经过焙烧以后，就会显现出某种固有的色泽。颜色釉分青釉、酱釉、黑釉、白釉、黄釉、绿釉、青白釉等几个大类，每种颜色还可以再细分。成色好的色釉瓷器以单纯、清丽、隽永而著称于世，给人以含蓄、内敛的美感。

- 景德镇窑青花山茶纹扁壶（明）
Flat Pot with Blue and White Camellia Pattern, Produced in Jingdezhen Kiln (Ming Dynasty 1368-1644)

- 景德镇窑粉彩莲花纹盖碗（清）
Famille Rose Tureen with Lotus Pattern, Produced in Jingdezhen Kiln (Qing Dynasty 1616-1911)

Four Major Porcelains of Jingdezhen

Blue-and-white porcelain, Rice-pattern Decorated porcelain, Famille Rose porcelain, Color-glazed porcelain are collectively referred to as Jingdezhen's four major porcelains.

Blue-and-white porcelain, first appeared in the Yuan Dynasty (1206-1368), is to draw the design with a pigment onto the stoneware body and paint over it with a transparent glaze and then fire it at a temperature of about 1,300 degrees Celsius. The crystal-clear glaze delivers an elegant, sober and low-key archaic flavor.

The Rice-pattern Decorated porcelain was created in the Xuande Period of the Ming Dynasty. It is to carve on the surface of the porcelain body many small holes and then fill in the glaze and fire. In the Qing Dynasty (1616-1911), porcelain workers cleverly combined it with Blue-and-white porcelain to create Exquisite Blue-and-white porcelain. Typically, Rice-pattern porcelain is decorated with blue and white design. The translucent patterns and the elegant blue and white design set off each other, lending the porcelain a clear and quaint note.

Famille Rose porcelain, known as *Ruancai* (meaning soft colors) porcelain, was introduced during the late reign of the Emperor Kangxi. It was so named due to its elegant and soft colors. Famille Rose porcelain features pastel shades, delicate and neat design, demonstrating a flavor of Chinese painting and strong national characteristics.

Reputed as "man-made gem", Color-glazed porcelain presents an inherent color by adding some kind of metal oxide in the glaze. Generally, it falls into the following categories: blue, dark reddish, black, white, yellow, green, blue-and-white glazed, and so on, with each color further subcategorized into specific types. First class color-glazed porcelain impresses with its pureness and elegance, and presents a subtle and restrained beauty.

湖南古镇

湖南省位于长江中游南岸,古称"潇湘",地处中国东南腹地,因全省大部分地处洞庭湖以南而得名"湖南"。湖南山川秀丽,名胜古迹众多。在湘南、湘西地区,更集中了很多保存完好的古镇、

Hunan Ancient Towns

Hunan Province, originally known as "Xiaoxiang", lies in the south of the middle Yangtze River valley, with its name meaning "south of the lake" because most of the province is located on the south of the Dongting Lake. Hunan is famous for its picturesque scenery.

古村落、古建筑。由于这些地区多是各民族杂居之地，因此在建筑上既有汉族风格，也有少数民族特色。

There are many places of historic interest and scenic beauty, including numerous well-preserved old towns, ancient villages and architecture in south and west of the province. These areas are mostly inhabited by multi-ethnic groups, so the architecture is of both Han and ethnic groups' styles.

● 夕阳下的洞庭湖 (图片提供：FOTOE)
洞庭湖位于湖南北部，是中国第四大湖，湖滨风光秀丽，名胜古迹众多。
Sunset on Dongting Lake
Dongting Lake, China's fourth largest lake, is located in the northern part of Hunan. The lakeside scenery is very beautiful, with a legion of historical sites and scenic spots.

湘绣锦鸡牡丹图轴（清）

湘绣是以湖南长沙为中心的刺绣产品的总称，主要以纯丝、硬缎、软缎、透明纱和各种颜色的丝线、绒线绣制而成。其特点是构图严谨，色彩鲜明，各种针法富有表现力，绣品形象生动，色彩鲜明，质感强烈，风格豪放。

Xiang Embroidery—Golden Pheasant and Peony, Hanging Scroll (Qing Dynasty 1616-1911)

Xiang embroidery refers to the embroidery product made in Changsha and surrounding areas. It is chiefly made of transparent chiffon silk, pure silk, hard and soft satin as well as silk threads and floss of various colors. The embroidery features rigorous composition and vivid colors; the diverse stitching techniques are expressive, and the patterns embroidered are of bright colors, strong textures and bold styles.

凤凰

凤凰又名"沱江镇"，位于湖南省西部土家族苗族自治州凤凰县，紧邻沱江而建。这里自古以来一直是苗族和土家族的聚居地，因境内的凤凰山而得名。

凤凰古城始建于清康熙四十三年（1704年），历经300多年的风雨沧桑，古貌犹存。城

Fenghuang

The old town of Fenghuang, also known as "The Town of Tuojiang River", is located in the county of the same name in Xiangxi Tujia and Miao Autonomous Prefecture on western boundary of Hunan Province. Built near Tuojiang River, Fenghuang has long been inhabited by the Miao and Tujia ethnic groups, and it takes its name from the Phoenix Mountain in the county.

Dating back to 1704, the town is in a good state of preservation after 300 years of trials and vicissitudes; the flagstone-paved streets, the wooden stilted houses by the river, and architectures such as

内青石板街道、江边木结构吊脚楼以及朝阳宫、杨家祠堂、天王庙、大成殿、万寿宫等建筑，无不具有古城特色。

　　凤凰古城分为新旧两个城区，老城依山傍水，清浅的沱江穿城而过，红色砂岩城墙伫立在岸边。北

Chaoyang Palace, the Yang's Ancestral Hall, Tianwang Temple, Dacheng Palace and the Palace of Longevity, etc., are permeated with the distinctive classical style of western Hunan.

　　Fenghuang consists of an old and a new district. The old Fenghuang at the foot of a hill is traversed by the clear

- 凤凰古城沱江边的古民居
  凤凰古城最有名的景观是一幢幢古色古香且富有土家族风情的吊脚楼。
  Ancient Dwellings by the Tuojiang River, Fenghuang
  The most famous landscape of Fenghuang is the stilted houses endowed with classic beauty and flavor of Tujia ethnic group.

城门下宽宽的河面上横着一条窄窄的木桥，以石为墩，两人对面要侧身而过，这里曾是当年出城的唯一通道。

凤凰古城明代时为五寨长官司治所，建有土城。明嘉靖三十五年（1556年），土城改建为砖城，开设四大门，各建城楼。到了清朝，古城的军事地位日显重

Tuojiang River, by which stands the city wall built of red sandstones. Below its northern gate a narrow wooden bridge lies across the broad river; with stone piers, it allows only one person to pass through at a time and used to be the only passage to the outside.

In the Ming Dynasty (1368-1644), the old Fenghuang was where the local government was located, and was

● 凤凰古城北门城楼
（图片提供：FOTOE）

The North Gate Tower , Fenghuang

要，古城的建设也得到加强。康熙五十四年（1715年），砖城改建为石城。古城墙气势宏伟，既有军事防御作用，又有城市防洪功能，成为古城的一道坚固屏障，虽几经战火，仍耸立于沱江河岸。古城墙北门城楼高约11米，名为"壁辉门"，采用本地产的红砂岩条石筑砌，建筑考究。砌墙的紫红砂石最重的达1200斤，轻的也有几百斤，伴以糯米粥与石灰灌浆砌筑，使城墙结构严密。两扇城门呈半月拱形，有铁皮包裹，上有密密麻麻的圆头大铁钉。城楼对外一面开有两层枪眼，每层4个，能防御城门外180度平面的区域。

虹桥又名"风雨楼"，是一座桥上有楼的大石桥，始建于明洪武七年（1374年），最初是由于沱江改道留下缺口而建的。清康熙九年（1670年），虹桥重建一次，为两台两墩三孔，因桥的两个桥墩呈船形，好像雨后彩虹横卧在沱江河上，故名"卧虹桥"。当时桥上两侧各建有12间悬出桥外的吊脚楼廊房，开设各种商店。1914年，沱江发生特大

surrounded by earth walls. In 1556 the walls were replaced by brick ones, with four gates built, each being surmounted by a gate tower. In the Qing Dynasty (1616-1911), the military status of the ancient city was becoming increasingly important, and the construction was also reinforced. In 1715, the brick walls were transformed into stone walls. The magnificent walls, reserved for both military defense and flood control, were a solid barrier of the ancient city; after several wars, they still stand by the Tuojiang River. The north gate tower is about 11 meters tall, and is called "Bihui Gate". It is carefully built of locally quarried stones laid with a mixture of sticky rice porridge and lime mortar, making them seamlessly joined. The stones used weigh from a few hundred pounds to 1,200 pounds. The gate is a semicircular arch; the two plates of the gate are wrapped by iron sheets and intensively nailed with iron rivets; there are two layers of four gun ports on the gate tower, capable of defending a 180° area outside the city gate.

Hongqiao Bridge (Rainbow Bridge), also known as "Wind and Rain Pavilion", is a big stone bridge capped with buildings. It was built in 1374, to

● 凤凰虹桥 (图片提供：FOTOE)
The Hong Bridge, Fenghuang

洪水，卧虹桥受到重创。后来凤凰人将此桥按原样整修，更名为"虹桥"。

德夯

德夯位于吉首市西郊20公里处，是苗族聚居地。"德夯"是苗语，意思是"美丽的峡谷"。德夯地处峡谷深处，山势跌宕，峰林重叠，形成了许多断崖、石壁、瀑布，风景十分优美。由于与外界交

bridge the gap caused by the diversion of Tuojiang River. In 1670, the bridge was rebuilt, with two terraces, two piers and three arches. It was formerly known as "Wohong Bridge" (Lying Rainbow Bridge) because its two boat-shaped piers look like a rainbow lying on the Tuojiang River. At that time there were 24 stilted corridors projecting from both sides of the bridge and serving as shops. In 1914 the bridge was seriously damaged by flood. Later it was restored by locals

通不便，许多苗家习俗都在这里得到了很好的保存。德夯的民居建筑统一为灰瓦木屋。水辗、古渡、小舟伴以苗家吊脚楼，一派田园风情。

to its original shape, and thus renamed "Hongqiao Bridge".

Dehang

Located 20 kilometers west of Jishou City, Dehang is an area inhabited by Miao ethnic group. "Dehang" is Miao language, meaning a beautiful canyon. The village is hidden deep in the valley, encircled by undulating mountains and overlapping peaks; the many precipices, cliffs and waterfall present to the eye a very picturesque view. Due to inconvenient transportation, many Miao customs here have been well preserved. All the residential buildings in the village are gray-tiled wooden huts. Waterwheels, an ancient ferry and little boats, accompanied by Miao-style stilted houses, form an idyllic pastoral scene.

By Yuquan Stream in front of Dehang Village, there is a stone peak towering into the sky, which is called "Tying Cattle Pillar". The stone peak is about 200 meters tall, and is grown with many old trees and giant vines, a scenery that may be called a manifestation of the uncanny craftsmanship of the Mother Nature. Not far from the peak stands a naturally formed "stone gate" about 350 meters tall, locally known as "Yuquan

• 德夯苗寨 (图片提供：FOTOE)
Miao Villages, Dehang

● 溪边的水车（图片提供：FOTOE）
Waterwheel by the Stream

德夯村寨前的玉泉溪畔，有一座青石峰直指云端，人称"苗家椎牛花柱"。石峰高200多米，呈方柱状，上多生古木巨藤，可谓鬼斧神工。椎牛花柱两侧不远处有一对天然形成的"石门"，有350多米高，人称"玉泉门"。玉泉门左右都是绝壁，上面生长着许多青松、灌木。玉泉门形成于五六亿年前的地质变化，如同两扇半开半掩的门。清澈的玉泉溪从这"门中"流出，

Gate"; the gate is flanked by cliffs, on which grow pine trees and shrubs. The Yuquan Gate, formed five or six hundred million years ago, resembles two semi-open doors. Clear stream flows through it, sliding down the stone steps to produce a beautiful trickling sound. Within the gate there is also a small pond with azure water.

Jielong Bridge of Dehang is a semicircular stone arch bridge, on both ends of which are flag-stone paved roads

接龙桥（图片来源：FOTOE）
Jielong Bridge

滑下石级，叮咚之声如拨琴弦。在玉泉门内还藏有一潭水，水色碧绿。

德夯接龙桥是一座半圆形的石拱桥，桥头两端接着由巨大青石板砌成的石板路，连起了夯峡溪两岸的苗寨。接龙桥是这里的苗民进行"接龙"活动的场所。到"接龙"那天，桥两侧和石板路两旁都插上彩旗，接龙队伍浩浩荡荡，充当"龙女"的人身着盛装、头戴插花银帽走在人群中间，身后是锣鼓、长号、唢呐队伍，热热闹闹从桥上走过，整个场面洋溢着浓郁的苗家乡土气息。

linking the Miao villages on both banks of the Hangxia Stream. The bridge is the place where the Miao people hold the folk activity "*Jielong*" (Dragon Chain). On that day, the bridge and the stone paths are decked with colorful flags; a team of villagers, with a person wearing splendid clothing and flower-studded caps in the middle of the crowd, walk vigorously across the bridge, followed by a row of suona players, percussionists and trombonists playing their instruments, a scene with strong local flavor of the Miao people.

> 东北古镇

中国东北地区包括黑龙江、吉林和辽宁三省。自明清以来，东北与中原之间的交流就十分频繁，各民族的混居交融使东北形成了具有特色的区域文化。东北古镇的建筑与民居极具地域风貌，以四合院式的庭院布局为主。

辽宁古镇

辽宁省自古以来多民族杂居，各民族在不同的地理环境、民族传统等因素影响下，形成了独特的文化风俗和民居形式。辽宁省现存的许多古镇，完好地保存着明清古建筑的原貌和特有的民族风情。

> Ancient Towns in Northeast China

Northeast China consists of three provinces: Heilongjiang, Jilin and Liaoning. Since the Ming and Qing dynasties, the people of the Northeast have had frequent exchanges with those from Central Plain; different ethnic groups live among one another and the Northeast has established a distinctive regional culture. The architecture of ancient towns in this area is of strong regional flavor and mostly of *Siheyuan*-style.

Liaoning Ancient Towns

Liaoning Province has since ancient times been inhabited by various ethnic groups. Influenced by different geographical environments, ethnic traditions and

永陵镇

永陵镇位于新宾满族自治县，是一个充满浓厚历史文化气息的古镇。早在新石器时代，这里就有人类居住。明代万历四十四年（1616年），努尔哈赤在今永陵镇东南的赫图阿拉城建立大金国，是为清朝的前身。清天聪八年（1634年），清太宗皇太极封赫图阿拉城为"兴京"，并开始修建兴京陵。顺治十六年（1659年），兴京陵被尊为"永陵"，永陵镇因此而得名。

永陵镇集中分布着许多清代前期的文物古迹，最著名的就是清朝12座帝陵中营建时间最早的清永陵建筑群。清永陵是清王朝的祖陵，陵内埋葬着清朝创立者努尔哈赤的六世祖、曾祖、祖父、父亲及他的伯父和叔父。陵寝前端为一条笔直的大道，称为"神道"。通过神道是清永陵的总门户"正红门"，其木栅栏的建筑形制保留了满族的建筑特色。永陵前院并列着清朝四位皇帝的碑亭，这在全国是独一无二的。永陵第二道门为启运门，通过启运门即方城，以启运殿为主体，

other factors, ethnic groups here have established their own unique cultural customs and type of dwellings. In many of the existing old towns of Liaoning, ancient buildings of the Ming and Qing dynasties and distinctive ethnic customs are well kept.

Yongling

Yongling, sitting in Xinbin Manchu Autonomous County, is an old town with strong historical and cultural atmosphere. As early as the Neolithic Age, there has been human habitation in this area. In 1616 of the Ming Dynasty, Nurhachi founded the Later Jin Dynasty in Hetu Ala—a place southeast of what is today's Yongling, the Later Jin Dynasty being the predecessor of the Qing Dynasty. In 1634, Hetu Ala was conferred the title "Xingjing" by Emperor Taizong who began to construct the Xingjing Tomb here. The tomb was crowned "Yongling Mausoleum" in 1659, hence the name Yongling.

In Yongling town there are a great many historic sites dated to the early Qing Dynasty, of which the most famous is the Yongling building complex—the oldest construction of the 12 mausoleums of Qing emperors. Yongling Mausoleum

左右两厢分置东西配殿，供奉着各位神灵。绕过启运殿就跨入宝城，是陵寝墓葬所在地，清王朝皇室的六位祖先就安息在这里。清永陵既具备皇家陵寝的传统格局，又保持了满族文化的本来面貌，是地方特色最浓郁的帝王陵寝建筑群。

is the tomb of Qing emperors' ancestors. Buried in there are Nurhachi's remote ancestors, great grandfather, grandfather, father and uncles. A straight road, known as Sacred Passage leads to the main gate of the mausoleum, whose wooden fence retains the architectural features of

● 清永陵四祖碑亭 (图片提供：FOTOE)
Four Ancestors' Stele Pavilions, Yongling Mausoleum

赫图阿拉城西距清永陵5公里,是一座拥有400余年历史的古城。"赫图阿拉"是满语,意为"横岗",即平顶小山冈。古城始建于明万历三十一年(1603年),万历四十四年(1616年)努尔哈赤在此称帝,建立了大金政权,史称"后金"。赫图阿拉城不仅是后金(清)开国的第一座都城,也是中国历史上最后一座山城式都城。作为后金政治、经济、军事、文化、外交的中心,赫图阿拉城被视为清王朝的发祥之地。赫图阿拉故城分内外两城,城垣由土、木、石杂筑而成。内城有各类后金宫殿、祠堂、衙署及文庙、关帝庙、城隍庙等古建筑和遗址,青砖青瓦,独具风格。

牛庄

牛庄镇隶属于辽宁鞍山海城市,位于海城河下游西岸。这里铁路、公路贯通,交通便利,水土肥美,自古就是周边地区的经济、文化中心。辽、金时期,辽河在这里附近入海,商船(时称"牛子")云集于此,故而得名"牛庄"。由于牛庄的经济和战略地位非常重

Manchu. In the front yard of Yongling Mausoleum stand four stele pavilions lined up in a row, unique in the whole country. The second gate of this complex is Qiyun Gate, inside which is the Square Castle consisting of Qiyun, the main hall and two side halls where divine tablets are located. Behind Qiyun Hall is the Treasure Castle—the location of tombs where six ancestors of the royal family of the Qing Dynasty rest in peace. Featuring both the traditional pattern of royal tombs and the original appearance of the Manchu culture, Yongling Mausoleum enjoys the strongest local flavor among all imperial tombs.

The city of Hetu Ala, located 5 kilometers west of Yongling Mausoleum, is a historical city with more than 400 years of history. Hetu Ala is "flat-topped hill" in Manchurian language, and the ancient city was built in 1603. In 1616 Nurhachi declared himself Khan (King) in Hetu Ala and founded the Later Jin Dynasty. Here was the first capital of the Later Jin Dynasty, and the last one in the form of mountain city in Chinese history. Hetu Ala is the political, economic, military, cultural, and diplomatic center of Later Jin Dynasty, and is considered the birthplace of the Qing Dynasty. It

• 赫图阿拉故城城垣 (图片提供：FOTOE)
City Wall, Old Hetu Ala

要，1623年，清太祖努尔哈赤曾命皇太极亲临牛庄犒赏筑城民夫，重筑牛庄城。咸丰八年（1858年），英、法、美、俄等国入侵天津，强迫清政府签订《天津条约》，牛庄被列入五个通商口岸之一，并于1861年4月正式开埠，成为东北地区最早开放的商埠。清末，牛庄镇内店铺、钱庄林立，吸引了许多国内

is comprised of inner and outer cities; the city wall is built of earth, wood, and stones; the inner city houses a large number of ancient buildings, such as various palaces of Later Jin, ancestral halls, government offices and the temples for Confucian, Guan Yu, the City God, etc.; all the buildings have gray-brick walls capped with gray tiles, a style that has a peculiar flavor of their own.

外商贾来牛庄兴业，镇内保留至今的有道光年间修建的太平桥、护城河以及法国传教士修建的天主教堂等独具特色的建筑。

- 清代末年的牛庄港口 (图片提供：FOTOE)
Niuzhuang Port, Constructed in Late Qing Dynasty

Niuzhuang

The town of Niuzhuang is part of Haicheng City, Liaoning Province, and it lies on the lower reaches of Haicheng River. With convenient transportation and fertile land, it has always been the economic and cultural center of the surrounding area. In the Liao (907-1125) and Jin (1115-1234) dynasties, the Liaohe River entered the sea somewhere nearby, and merchant ships (known as "calves" at the time) gathered here, hence the name Niuzhuang (calf village). In 1623 Nurhachi ordered the reconstruction of Niuzhuang, as it had a significant strategic position and abundant economic resources. In 1858, Britain, France, America, Russia and other countries invaded Tianjin, forcing the Qing government to sign the *Treaty of Tianjin*. Niuzhuang, included in the five treaty ports, was formally opened in April 1861, becoming the earliest commercial port in the Northeast region. Towards the end of the Qing Dynasty, Niuzhuang was crowded with shops and banks, attracting many domestic and foreign merchants. The buildings preserved today include Taiping Bridge and the city moat constructed during the Daoguang

太平桥位于牛庄镇北关，又称"北关石桥"，建于清道光二十八年（1848年）。石桥长50米、宽4.5米，桥洞15孔。该桥桥墩和桥面完全采用花岗岩筑成，虽历经百年，仍然十分坚固。桥两侧的立柱上雕刻着各种吉祥图案，有石狮、石猴、水果等，每样都刻得惟妙惟肖。

太平桥西边是观音寺旧址，俗称"老母庙"，是牛庄旧时香火

Period of the Qing Dynasty, and unique architecture such as the Catholic Cathedral built by French missionaries.

Located in Beiguan of Niuzhuang, Taiping Bridge also known as Beiguan Stone Bridge was constructed in 1849, with a length of 50 meters, a width of 4.5 meters and 15 arches. The piers and deck of the bridge, completely built of granite, are still sturdy after a century; the balustrades on both sides are carved with

- 牛庄太平桥
  Taiping Bridge, Niuzhuang

鼎盛的大庙之一。老观音寺建于清朝初年，嘉庆十二年（1807年）重修。旧时每年农历二月十九的观音圣诞日，观音寺都会举办法会和庙会，热闹非凡。

all kinds of auspicious patterns: lions, monkeys, fruits, etc., all done skillfully and vividly.

　　To the west of Taiping Bridge is the Temple of Avalokitesvara, Commonly known as Laomu Temple, which used to be a large temple attracting lots of worshippers and pilgrims in old times. It was built in the early Qing Dynasty and rebuilt in 1807. In the past, on the 19th of the second month of lunar calendar—the birthday of Avalokitesvara, the temple would be crowded with people who flocked to take part in the religious rites and temple fair held here.

> 华北古镇

华北地区自元至清都是封建王朝都城所在地，因此华北的古镇建筑大都气势威严、高大宏伟，于粗犷中不失细腻，彰显出四平八稳的气度。

山西古镇

山西省是中华民族的发祥地之一，早在250万年以前，这里就已经有了早期的原始人类。山西地区由于是中原与北方游牧民族活动区域的交界地带，自古地位举足轻重。明清时期，山西商人崛起，到清朝中晚期更占据了全国金融界的领导地位。在晋中地区的古镇，至今仍保存着不少当年晋商留下的深宅大

> Ancient Towns in North China

From the Yuan and Qing dynasties onwards, North China was where the dynastic capitals situated. In this area, the buildings in ancient towns are mostly imposing and majestic. Rough yet delicate, these buildings are stable and square.

Shanxi Ancient Towns

Shanxi Province is one of the birthplaces of the Chinese nation. As early as 2.5 million years ago, there has been early hominid living here. Shanxi region is the border between the Central Plains and the area inhabited by the nothern nomadic people, and holds an important position since ancient times. Shanxi merchants rose in the Ming and Qing dynasties, and

院，体现出晋商的雄厚实力，而且处处蕴涵着传统封建礼教的意味。

in the mid and late Qing Dynasty they dominated Chinese financial business. In ancient towns of Jinzhong region, there are many well-preserved courtyard houses left by Shanxi merchants, which reflects the strong economic strength of those merchants and also imply the significance of the traditional feudal ethics.

- **山西祁县乔家大院**
  山西祁县的乔家大院是清末民初大晋商乔致庸的宅第，始建于清嘉庆年间，后经数次增修扩建，占地约8724平方米，分为6个大院，内套20个小院，共313个房间。大院四周砖墙高约12米，显得威严气派，建筑装饰设计精巧、工艺繁复，体现了清代民居建筑的最高水平。

  Qiao's Grand Courtyard of Qixian County, Shanxi Provice
  The Qiao's Grand Courtyard was the private residence of Qiao Zhiyong, the famous merchant active in the late Qing and early Minguo Period. Built in the Jiaqing Period of the Qing Dynasty and later expanded several times, this compound covers about 8,724 square meters of land, consisting of 20 small yards set in 6 large ones with 313 rooms in total. The dignified wall of the compound is about 12 meters tall; its architectural design and decoration is delicate and complicated, and is considered the finest example of residential buildings in the Qing Dynasty.

● 黄河壶口瀑布 (图片提供：FOTOE)
Hukou Waterfall of the Yellow River

平遥

　　平遥始建于西周，至今已有2800年的历史，是一座完全按照中国传统规划思想和布局设计修建的城镇。1997年，平遥被联合国教科文组织列为世界文化遗产。

　　平遥古城共有四大街、八小街、七十二道窄巷，是由完整的古民居、古城墙、古街巷、古庙宇组

Pingyao

Built in the Western Zhou Dynasty (1046 B.C.-771 B.C.), Pingyao has a history of 2,800 years, and is totally based on the Chinese traditional planning and layout. In 1997, Pingyao was listed as a UNESCO World Heritage Site.

　　With four avenues, eight streets and 72 alleys, the old city of Pingyao is a large architectural complex composed

成的大型古建筑群，基本保持了明清时期的民居风貌。

明朝初年，为加强军事防御，平遥始建城墙。清康熙四十三年（1704年），因康熙西巡路经平遥，城墙遂又加筑了四面大城楼，

of ancient residential houses, city walls, streets and temples, which basically retain the features of the Ming and Qing dynasties.

Construction of city walls of Pingyao started in the early Ming Dynasty as a fortification. In 1704, four great gate towers were added to the walls at the behest of Emperor Kangxi during his tour to the west. The walls have six gates; one gate each on the north and south sides, and two apiece on the east and west sections. Seen from above, this pattern is similar to that of a turtle: the south gate of the city as the head, the two wells outside the gate as the eyes and the north gate —the lowest point of the whole city— as the tail. Turtle is an animal symbolic of longevity, and local people hope that it will bring permanent security to the old city of Pingyao.

• **平遥古城墙**

平遥城墙高12米、宽5米、周长6163米，环周共有72座堞楼、3000个垛口，是国内现存最完整的古城墙之一。

Old City Wall of Pingyao

The wall is about 12 meters high and 5 meters wide, with a perimeter of 6,163 meters. There are also 72 watchtowers and 3,000 battlements on the wall, making it one of the most complete old walls that have survived in China.

• 平遥古城古市楼
　The Ancient City of Pingyao

更加壮观。鸟瞰平遥古城，平面方形的城墙形如龟状，城门六座，南北各一，东西各二。城池南门为龟首，门外两眼水井象征龟的双目。北城门为龟尾，是全城的最低处，城内所有积水都要经此流出。乌龟属长寿动物，在古人心目中如同神灵，当地人希冀平遥古城坚如磐石、永世长存。

　　The Temple of the City God, located in the east of the old city, is an age-old Taoist Temple. It was built in the early Ming Dynasty and renovated in 1864 in the Qing Dynasty. The extant buildings in the temple are of Qing style, with magnificent courtyard and a complete and orderly layout. Built facing south, the compound has a succession of four yards composed of Temple of the City God,

● 平遥城隍庙
Temple of the City God, Pingyao

平遥城隍庙是一座年代久远、规制齐全的官祀道教庙宇,位于平遥古城东侧。城隍庙始创于明初,在清同治三年（1864年）重修,现存建筑属于清代规制,庙院宏大,布局完整,整个建筑群坐北朝南,前后四进院落,由城隍庙、财神庙、灶君庙以及真武楼等组成。总体布局既有寺庙建筑的特色,又有官署建筑的意趣。

票号是清代出现的一种私人金融机构,专营银钱的异地汇兑和存放款业务。位于平遥古城西大街

Temple of the God of Fortune, Temple of Kitchen God and Zhenwu Pavilion. The overall layout has the features of both Taoist architecture and official residences.

Exchange shops are private financial institutions appeared in the Qing Dynasty (1616-1911), engaging in money exchanges, deposits and loans. The Rishengchang (Sunrise Prosperity) Exchange Shop, founded in 1823 as one of the earliest exchange shops in China, is located in the busy section of West Street in Pingyao City. Owing much to the smart management and good reputation, the yearly exchange amount of the shop

繁华地段的日升昌票号是中国第一家票号，创于1823年。由于经营灵活、注重信誉，在鼎盛时期，年汇兑金额高达3800万两白银，经营票号几乎遍布整个中国。

日升昌票号旧址至今保存完好，共有三进院落，坐南朝北，整个院落墙高宅深，布局紧凑，设计精巧，上空架设有铁丝网，网上系有响铃，用于防盗。

双林寺原名"中都寺"，始建于南北朝时期，北宋时改名双林

was up to 38 million taels of silver in its heyday, and its business branches were established almost throughout China.

The former Rishengchang Exchange Shop is in a good state of preservation. Facing south, it has a succession of three sections; the whole complex, compactly designed, is surrounded by high walls, on which barbed wire fences with alarms are mounted.

Shuanglin Temple, formerly "Zhongdu Temple", was built in the Northern and Southern dynasties (420-589), and got

- 日升昌票号旧址
  The Former Rishengchang Exchange Shop

• 双林寺中的自在观音像 (图片提供：FOTOE)

这尊自在观音像右腿曲蹲，左脚轻踏荷叶，右手微翘，左手支撑，一副无拘无束、自由自在的样子。

The Statue of Avalokitesvara, Shuanglin Temple

The figrue of the statue is seated, curling right leg and placing the left foot gently on a lotus leave; one of hands supports the body, while the other rests on knee. The statue looks relaxed and carefree.

寺。明代及清道光、宣统年间，该寺都有过较大的修葺。寺院规模宏大，殿内现存宋、元、明、清时期的大小彩塑2052尊，包括佛、观音、金刚、罗汉等塑像，每座都形神兼备、生动传神，是难得的古代艺术珍品。

碛口

碛口古镇位于吕梁市临县，地处晋陕黄河大峡谷的中段，自古就是军事要冲。在明清至民国年间，碛口凭黄河水运一跃成为北方著名

its name "Shuanglin" in the Northern Song Dynasty (960-1127). In the Ming and late Qing dynasties, it went through large scale renovations. The giant temple houses 2,052 painted sculptures of varied sizes made in the Song, Yuan, Ming and Qing dynasties, including the statues of Buddha, Avalokitesvara, guardian warriors and arhats, etc., each with vivid expression and lively posture, indeed the art treasure of ancient times.

Qikou

Located in Linxian County, Lvliang City, the old town of Qikou is in the middle of the "Shanxi-Shaanxi Gorge" section of the Yellow River, and has been a military hub since old times. From Ming and Qing dynasties down to the Minguo Period, Qikou became a famous commercial center of North China by virtue of its water transport on the Yellow River,

的商贸重镇，享有"九曲黄河第一镇"的美誉。

碛口因临近黄河大同碛而得名。"碛"，本义为水中的沙石，这里指黄河上因地形起伏而形成的一段段激流浅滩。大同碛位于碛口古街西南500米的湫水河入黄河处，是秦晋峡谷间最大的一个碛。黄河进入大同碛，河面急剧收缩为百米

earning itself the accolade "No.1 Town by the Yellow River".

Qikou takes its name from the Datong *Qi* of the Yellow River. *Qi* refers to a section of whitewater shoals formed on the Yellow River due to the undulating terrain. Datong *Qi*, sitting where the Qiushui River meets the Yellow River, 500 meters southwest of Qikou Old Street, is the biggest shoal in the Shanxi-

- 黄河边的碛口古镇 (图片提供: FOTOE)
  The Old Town of Qikou by the Yellow River

左右，河水涌向落差约10米、长3000米的倾斜河道，水流湍急、咆哮如雷。黄河因大同碛而受阻，但碛口的繁荣却正是缘于大同碛。由于船筏难以通行，碛口成为黄河北干流上水运航道的中转站。鼎盛时

- **碛口镇上的古老街巷** (图片提供：FOTOE)

  碛口镇的街道用石头铺砌，依地形曲折蜿蜒，街道两旁的店铺、民居多为明清时期的建筑。

  Ancient Streets and Lanes in Qikou

  In Qikou Town, the stone-paved streets wind their way up and down; the shops and residences along the streets are mostly built in the Ming and Qing dynasties.

Shaaxi Gorge. On entering into the Datong *Qi*, the Yellow River is narrowed sharply to about one hundred meters; fast-flowing water roars like thunder, flowing down a 3,000-meter sloping river course with a 10-meter drop. Qikou owed much of its prosperity to Datong *Qi* although the latter somewhat blocks the Yellow River. Hard for boats to pass through, Qikou became a transit station between land and water transport north of the Yellow River. During its heyday, hundreds of boats berthed at the port

卧虎山上的黑龙庙
Heilong Temple on the Wohu Mountain

期，碛口码头每天来往的船只达150艘之多，各类店铺300多家。镇内现存大量保存完好的明清时期建筑，主要有货栈、票号、当铺等各类商业性建筑，还有庙宇、民居、码头等，镇上居民也保持着原始质朴的生活形态，所以碛口被称为"活着的古镇"。

碛口镇卧虎山上的黑龙庙创建于明代，清雍正年间修建乐楼，道光年间再次重修，规模宏大，气势壮观。作为碛口镇的标志性建筑，黑龙庙踞于黄河边的高处，居高临下，具有一

every day, and more than 300 shops of various kinds were established in the town. Today, the town has a great number of well-preserved architectures of the Ming and Qing dynasties, ranging from warehouses, exchange shops, pawnshops and other types of commercial buildings to temples, residences and ports. The residents in the town still maintain their traditional way of life, hence it is known as the "Living Old Town".

On a mountain near Qikou Town there is a temple named Heilong (Black Dragon), which was built in the Ming

种威严的气势。历史上，当地人的祈雨活动都在这里进行，香火鼎盛。黑龙庙整体建筑严谨合理，左右对称，正殿内供奉着传说中负责降雨的神明黑龙大王。

李家山村为明清时期的李氏家族所建，村里民居以窑洞为主，随着山坡高低错落，窑洞前普遍有廊檐伸出，形成四合院。整个民居群分布在黄土山坡上，较大的四合院建筑均以水磨砖对缝砌筑，造型风格十分考究。窑

Dynasty and added with an opera stage in the Yongzheng Period of the Qing Dynasty. Rebuilt in the Daoguang Period of the Qing Dynasty, the temple is magnificent and spectacular. As the landmark building of Qikou Town, the Heilong Temple stands high on the hill, overlooking the Yellow River in an imposing manner. Historically, the locals prayed for rain here, so the temple had lots of worshippers and pilgrims. It is judicously designed and symmetric along a central axis; in the main hall is enshrined the Dragon King, who according to legend is responsible for the rainfall.

Lijiashan Village was established by the Li family of Ming and Qing dynasties. The village is located on loess slopes; residential buildings in the village are chiefly cave dwellings, which undulate following the fall and rise of the terrain. The cave houses generally have projecting verandas and wing rooms to form a courtyard. Large courtyard buildings are built of bath bricks, with an extremely

• 李家山村的窑洞民居 (图片提供：FOTOE)
Cave Dwellings in Lijiashan Village

洞门窗上的砖木雕刻比比皆是，图案包括人物、山水、花鸟鱼虫、飞禽走兽等，十分精美。

河南古镇

河南省地处中原，是中华文明的重要发祥地之一，有着十分丰富的古代文化遗存。在河南各地的古镇中，民居建筑类型丰富多样，如豫东、豫北地区的四合院，豫西地区的窑洞建筑等，展现了高超的建筑技术与深厚的文化内涵。

朱仙镇

朱仙镇位于河南省开封市西南，自唐宋以来，一直是水陆交通要道和商埠之地。明朝时，作为开封唯一的水陆转运码头，朱仙镇迅速繁荣起来，到明末，朱仙镇已名列全国四大名镇，镇中民商有4万余户，人口达20多万。贾鲁河从镇里南北穿过，把全镇分为东西两部分。河上的大石桥和二板桥又把全镇联成一体，镇内保留着不少古色古香的旧式建筑，整个集镇显得幽雅、别致。

朱仙镇的岳飞庙建于明成化年

exquisite shape and style; brick and wood carvings can be found on every door and window; the patterns, including figures, landscapes, flowers, fish and insects, birds and beasts, are very beautiful.

Henan Ancient Towns

Located on the Central Plains, Henan Province is one of the birthplaces of Chinese civilization, and is rich in ancient cultural relics. In old towns across Henan, the residential buildings are of various types, such as the courtyard houses in east and north of Henan, cave dwellings in western part of the province, all demonstrating superior construction techniques and profound cultural connotations.

Zhuxian Town

Zhuxian Town sits southwest of Kaifeng City, Henan Province. Since the Tang and Song dynasties, it has been the hub of land and water transportation and a commercial port. In the Ming Dynasty(1368-1644), as the only land and water transit terminal in Kaifeng, Zhuxian Town quickly flourished, and down to the late Ming, it has been one of the "Four Top Towns" around the country, with more than 40,000 civil merchants and

● 朱仙镇古桥 (图片提供：FOTOE)
Ancient Bridge of Zhuxian Town

a population of over 200,000. The Jialu River runs through the town and divides it into two sections, which are connected by two bridges. Elegant and unique, the town houses many ancient buildings that exude classic beauty.

Constructed between 1465 and 1487, the Yue Fei Temple in Zhuxian Town faces south and has a succession of three courtyards; the side corridor around the courtyards is of rectangular shape. In the majestic and imposing compound there are numerous stele pavilions and a variety of carvings, painted sculptures and iron casting statues. Enshrined in the main hall are the statues of Yue Fei and his family members for worshiping and revering; the kneeling iron statues in the yard are the traitor minister Qin Hui, his wife and other treacherous officials whom people spit upon and revile. The temple went through many renovations in the Ming and Qing dynasties, and still attracts a lot of worshippers and pilgrims.

In the Ming and Qing dynasties, some Muslim merchants from home and abroad came to Zhuxian Town for

间（1465—1487），坐北向南，为三进院落，外廊呈长方形，整个殿堂恢宏庄严，碑亭林立，刻绘塑铸作品丰富多彩。大殿中有岳飞及其家人的塑像供人景仰、祭拜，院中还有秦桧夫妇和奸臣的跪像，供人唾骂。岳飞庙历经明清两代多次整修，香火十分旺盛。

明清时期，一些中外穆斯林商贾来到朱仙镇进行商品贸易，在此地修建了7座清真寺，其中的北寺（即朱仙镇清真寺）保存最完好。朱仙镇清真寺建筑最大的特点就是既有明清时期建筑特色，又有浓厚的民族色彩。

朱仙镇木版年画是中国四大木版年画之一，历来为国内外美术界所敬慕。朱仙镇年画起源于唐代，兴于宋代，鼎盛于明清，历史悠久，其制作采用木版与镂版相结合的方法，水印套色，种类繁多。年画的题材和内容大多取材于历史戏剧、演义小说、神话故事和民间传说，构图饱满，线条简练，造型古朴，色彩艳丽，人物普遍

merchandise trade, and they built seven mosques here, of which the North Temple (Mosque in Zhuxian Town) is the best preserved one. What is prominent is that it is a hybrid of architecture of Ming and Qing Dynasties and the Muslim mosque.

Woodblock New Year picture of Zhuxian Town is one of the four major Chinese woodblock New Year pictures and has always been admired by fine art circles at home and abroad. Originating

• 朱仙镇清真寺 (图片提供: FOTOE)
Mosque in Zhuxian Town

● 朱仙镇年画《五子登科》
New Year Picture of Zhuxian Town *Five Sons Passing the Imperial Examination*

in the Tang Dynasty, prospering in the Song Dynasty and flourishing in the Ming and Qing dynasties, it boasts rich varieties, pressed with a combination of embossed and hollowed planks, in a manner of water mark color process. The subjects and contents of New Year pictures are mostly based on historical dramas, romance novels, fairy tales and folklore. Vibrantly colored, full of rounded and fulsome figures and animals, these pictures are permeated with rich local color and flavor. Figures, generally with big heads and small bodies, appear comic.

Jingziguan

Located at the juncture of the three provinces—Henan, Hubei and Shaanxi, the town of Jingziguan is a part of Xichuan County, Henan Province. Due to the difficult terrain, it has been a military hub and commerce center since old times. As early as the Western Han Dynasty (206 B.C.-25 A.D.), Jingziguan was a small bazaar, originally known as "Caoqiaoguan" (the Straw-bridge Pass). In the mid-Tang Dynasty, a lot of goods in the South were to be transported through the Danjiang River to Chang'an, the bustling capital of Tang.

头大身子小，既有喜剧效果又体现出浓郁的乡土气息和地方色彩。

荆紫关

荆紫关镇隶属于河南省淅川县，位于豫、鄂、陕三省结合部，素有"一脚踏三省"之称。由于地势险要，这里自古就是兵家必争的要塞和商贸繁盛之地。早在西汉时期，荆紫关即成小集，始名"草桥关"。唐朝中叶，京都长安鼎盛，南方许多物资都要通过丹江运往长安。荆紫关随着航运和商业的兴盛

而进一步繁华起来，逐渐形成集镇，称为"荆子关"。清朝时期，荆子关的河运空前繁荣，码头上每天停泊各类船只百余艘，荆子关成

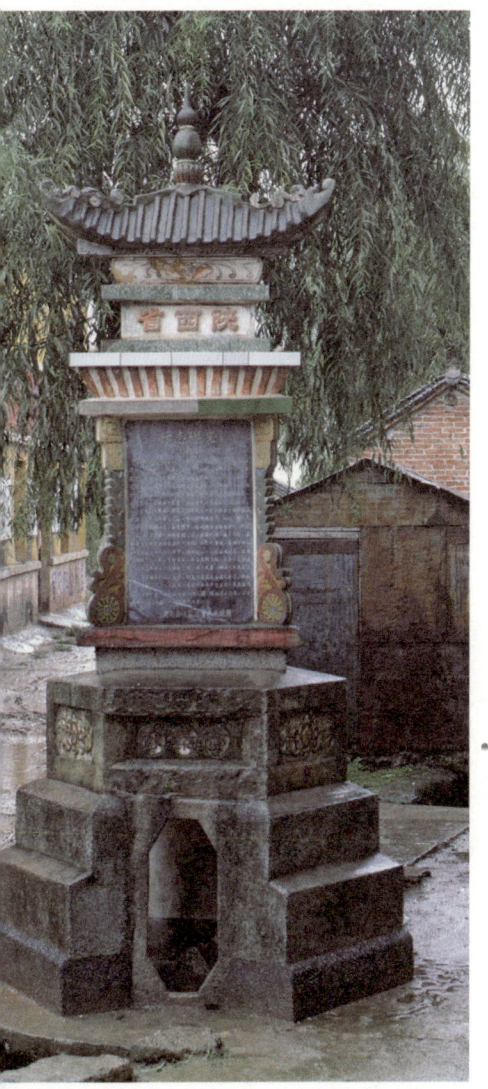

Taking this opportunity, Jingziguan saw a further flourish and gradually became a market town. In the Qing Dynasty, water transport in Jingziguan experienced an unprecedented prosperity, hundreds of boats of various sizes berthing at the port every day. The town became a cargo hub of its surrounding areas, and merchants from various regions gathered here doing business. In the early Minguo Period, Jingziguan took its present name from the auspicious meaning of "The Purple Air comes from the east—a propitious omen."

The "Qing Dynasty Street" in the town is one of the best-preserved ancient streets in north China. The old street, encircled by mountains and rivers and comprised of North and South

● **荆紫关三省交界碑** (图片提供·FOTOE)

这块碑有3米多高，呈三面棱柱状，三面依次有河南、陕西、湖北三省所书的碑文。碑下有一块露出地面的三棱尖石，一面朝西，一面朝东南，一面朝东北，被称为"一脚踏三省"石。

The Three-provinces Boundary Marker in Jingziguan

In shape of triangular prism, this boundary marker is 3 meters tall; on its three sides are carved inscriptions by Henan, Shaanxi, Hubei provinces respectively. Below the boundary marker is a stone that looks like triangular pyramid, with the three sides facing west, southeast and northeast, known as "a foot stepping on three provinces".

为方圆百里的货物集散中心，各地商人云集于此。民国初年，为取"紫气东来"的吉祥含义，荆子关改称"荆紫关"，沿用至今。

镇中保存完好的"清代一条街"是中国北方目前保存最完好的古街之一。该街分为南、中、北三街，每一条街都是直街，街与街之间有斜弯相连。古老的街道被山水环拱，融合了南北建筑风格，显得古朴而独特。长约2500米的古街道两旁，现存700余间清代建筑，基本维持原貌。街道上的房舍，一般临街的都是店铺的门面房，房门由漆成黑色的一块块木板组成，白天卸下、夜晚装上，十分方便。里面多是两到三进的小院，可以容纳一家三代、四代居住。每一个院落门面房两侧的前坡都有1米多长的"防火墙"，可在邻家发生火灾时隔绝蔓延的火势。古街的居民在防火墙上加以彩绘和雕刻，使之不仅为房屋防火设施，更成为一种装饰构件。

平浪宫是荆紫关古建筑群中较为壮观的一座，建于清崇德三年（1638年）。在荆紫关码头极盛

architectural styles, demonstrates an antique and unique atmosphere. It is divided into three sections: south, middle and north streets, each being a straight street; the three are linked by curved lanes. Along both sides of the 2,500-meter street sit 700-plus buildings of the Qing Dynasty that are basically untouched. In the street, shops were generally built fronting the street; their doors were made of wooden boards painted black, taken down during the day and mounted at night. Behind the shops were usually small compounds with two or three yards, capable of accommodating a household with three or four generations. In every residence a wall was erected in front of the gate to prevent fire from spreading into the compound; besides blocking fire, these walls were added with colored patterns or carvings by locals to make them a decorative element of the compound.

Among the ancient architecture in Jingziguan, Pinglang Palace (Pinglang means gentle breezes and calm waves), built in 1638, is a spectacular one. In the heyday of Jingziguan port, boat owners built this palace, hoping the auspicious meaning of its name would bring safety to their sailing, and the palace became the

● 荆紫关的清代老街 (图片提供：FOTOE)
Old Street Dated to Qing Dynasty, Jingziguan

时期，船商们组建船帮，取"风平浪静"之意，筹建了平浪宫，成为船工娱乐、集会之地。该宫坐东向西，面对丹东，中轴线上现存大门楼、中宫、后宫及配房数间，另有钟鼓楼各一座，建筑风格富有陕南特色。

place where boatmen held recreational activities or rallies. The palace faces east toward Dandong; the existing buildings along the central axis include a great gate tower, middle hall, rear hall, two bell and drum towers, and several wing rooms. The architectural style is of rich flavors of Southern Shaanxi.

> 西北古镇

西北地区包括陕西、甘肃、宁夏、青海等地，地域广阔，民族众多，西北古镇的民风民俗和民居类型更是丰富多彩。由于西北大部分地区干旱少雨，古镇中的建筑多属于土木结构的平顶房，就地取材，建造成本低廉，追求一种实用、简朴的建筑风格。

陕西古镇

陕西省古称"关中"，据考证，中国最早的房屋建筑便出现在这块土地上。经过了千百年的变迁，陕西古镇形成了独有的古朴恢宏的建筑风格，其布局及空间处理比较严谨，多数为传统的四合院、三合院，院落层次较多，颇具气势。

> Ancient Towns in Northwest China

The northwest region, including Shaanxi, Gansu, Ningxia, Qinghai and other provinces and regions, has a vast territory and many ethnic groups. Ancient towns in this area are also rich in folk customs and house types. As most of the region has very limited rainfall, the buildings in old towns are mainly flat-topped housing built of local materials such as earth and wood. Such houses deliver a practical and simple architectural style, and the making of them did not cost much.

Shaanxi Ancient Towns

Shaanxi Province was formerly known as "Guanzhong". According to research, the earliest housing construction of China appeared in this place. After thousands

青木川

青木川位于陕西省西南部的宁强县境内，地处陕、甘、川三省交界处、秦岭余脉的大山中，是陕西省最西的一个古镇。据考证，青木川建造于明朝中叶，成型于清朝中后期，鼎盛于民国，是羌族和汉族杂居地区。青木川曾是入川的要道之一，也是商贾云集的边贸重镇。历经百年沧桑，青木川至今仍保存着大量风格迥异的古街、古祠、古栈道、古建筑群等历史古迹。

• 青木川镇鸟瞰 (图片提供：FOTOE)
  Bird's Eye View of Qingmuchuan

of years of changes, the ancient town of Shaanxi has formed a unique, simple and magnificent architectural style; these towns are carefully laid out, and mostly comprised of traditional courtyard houses surrounded by buildings on three or four sides; the houses often contain many courtyards, which look majestic and imposing.

Qingmuchuan

Qingmuchuan of Ningqiang County in the southwest of Shaanxi Province is located in Qinling Mountains at the junction of Shaanxi, Gansu and Sichuan provinces. It is the westernmost ancient town in Shaanxi Province. According to research, Qingmuchuan, where Qiang and Han people inhabit, originated in

● 青木川镇老街 (图片提供：FOTOE)
Ancient Street of Qingmuchuan

青木川镇的古建筑主要分布在回龙场街两旁。该街始建于明成化年间（1465—1487），街道建筑自下而上蜿蜒延伸八百多米，沿着金溪河绕着古镇形成弧状，好似一条卧龙，现留有古建筑房屋260间，雕梁画栋，古朴典雅。

榆林

榆林，又称"驼城"，位于陕西省最北部，地处黄土高原与毛乌素沙漠的交接地带，地域广阔，

the mid-Ming Dynasty, took shape in the Qing Dynasty (1616-1911) and flourished in the Minguo Period (1912-1949). Qingmuchuan used to be the main passage to Sichuan and an important trade center in the border region. After a hundred years, it still houses a large number of ancient streets, ancestral halls, ancient plank roads and ancient buildings of different styles.

The ancient buildings of Qingmuchuan are chiefly represented by those in Huilongchang Street, constructed between

地貌独特。万里长城横贯其中，以长城为界，长城以北为广阔无际的风沙草滩，长城以南是黄土丘陵，沟壑纵横。榆林最初只是一个居民点，因当地有普惠泉，四周榆树丛生，人们围泉而居，称为"榆林庄"。明代，榆林逐渐成为北方的军事重镇，范围也逐步扩大。今天的榆林保留着很多建于明清时代的衙署、府邸、庙宇、店铺等，一般民居多采用四合院形式，灰砖院

1465 and 1487. The 800-meter inclined street, following the curve of the Jinxi River to form an arc around the town, is lined with buildings, which is like a lying dragon when seen from afar. Today, about 260 simple and elegant ancient houses lie in the street, which are richly carved and ornamented.

Yulin

Yulin, also called "Camel City", is the northernmost city of Shaanxi province, and lies where the Loess Plateau and the

- 榆林古城老街 (图片提供：FOTOE)
Ancient Street of Yulin

• 榆林古城墙 (图片提供：FOTOE)
Ancient City Wall of Yulin

落、斑驳的影壁、木制雕花窗、锈迹斑斑的铜门环，展现出古朴厚重的明清风貌。

　　始建于明洪武二年（1369年）的榆林城墙，距今已有600多年的历史，是国内现存为数不多的极具地方特色的古城墙。榆林城墙在明代曾经过多次拓建，到万历三十

Ordos Desert meet. With vast territory and unique landforms, it is cut through by the Great Wall, to the north of which is boundless sand marsh while loess hills and ravines to the south. Yulin, originally a residential area, was formerly known as "Yulin Zhuang" (Village of Elm Trees) for the fact that there was a spring surrounded by clusters of elm trees which

年（1602年）城垣建成时，周长有6000多米，出于军事需要，城墙高度超过了北京城墙。清代，古城墙又经过多次修筑加固。同治二年（1863年），榆林城北墙被流沙积压，遂将北城墙向西南回缩，形成今日所见榆林的样子。

凌霄塔是榆林的标志性建筑，位于榆林城南，始建于明正德十年（1515年），原为榆阳寺中之塔，寺庙在清同治年间（1862—1874

later drew hordes of people residing here. In the Ming Dynasty (1368-1644), Yulin gradually became a military stronghold in the north, its territory being increasingly expanded. Today Yulin still abounds in buildings of Ming and Qing dynasties, such as government offices, official residences, temples and shops. Common residential buildings mostly appear as courtyard houses; the gray-brick courtyard, mottled screen wall, carved wooden windows and rusty copper knockers demonstrate the quaint and stately styles and features of the Ming and Qing dynasties.

The city wall of Yulin started its construction in 1369. Dating back over 600 years, it is one of the few extant ancient walls with rich local characteristics in China. The wall was expanded several times in the Ming Dynasty, and upon completion in 1602, it had a circumference of over 6,000 meters. For defense reasons, it was higher than its counterpart in Beijing. In the Qing Dynasty, the ancient city wall was reinforced many times. In 1863, the northern part of the wall was buried by drift sand, so a new section was built westward of the original, and this is what we see today.

● 凌霄塔
Lingxiao Pagoda

被毁，只有塔留存下来。凌霄塔为楼阁式八角形砖砌空心结构，共有13层，高43米。塔身每层砖雕仿木斗拱脚檐，檐角挂有风铃，迎风叮当作响。塔顶覆有琉璃碧瓦。在塔的最底层四面开门，由下往上，每层各面皆开有一窗。塔内有砖阶和木梯，游人可拾级而上，登上塔顶，榆林全城尽收眼底。

Lingxiao Pagoda, standing south of Yulin, is a landmark building of the city. Constructed in 1515 of the Ming Dynasty, it was formerly part of the Yuyang Temple; although the latter was destroyed in the Qing Dynasty, the pagoda has survived. The 43-meter octagonal brick pagoda is of hollow structure with thirteen tiers of eaves. On each tier of the pagoda there are brick carvings in imitation of wooden brackets and corner eaves; wind-bells are hung under the corner of the eaves, tinkling and jingling whenever there is breeze. The roof is covered with green glazed tiles. The ground floor of the pagoda has doors opening in four directions, and on the upper floors there are windows on all eight sides of the pagoda, one for each side. Brick steps and wooden ladders were built inside the pagoda. Climbing up the stairs and overlooking from the top, one would have a panoramic view of Yulin city.

> 华南古镇

华南地区的古镇有着鲜明的地方特色和个性特征，蕴涵着丰富的文化内涵，除了注重实用功能外，还十分注重自身的空间形式、艺术风格、民俗传统以及与周围环境的协调。

福建古镇

福建省简称"闽"，位于中国东南沿海地区，气候温和，雨量充沛，森林覆盖率居全国首位。公元前221年，秦置闽中郡，从此福建作为一个行政区出现在中国版图上。福建自古就有多民族定居，由于战乱等原因，大批客家人迁入福建，他们给福建带来了独具特色的文化，福建古镇建筑就充分体现了这

> Ancient Towns in South China

Old towns in South China have distinctive local characteristics and their own traits, containing rich cultural connotations. In addition to functions, they pay more attention to their own spatial forms, artistic styles, folk traditions and their harmony with surrounding environment.

Fujian Ancient Towns

Fujian Province, "Min" for short, is located in the southeast coast of China. It has a mild climate and abundant rainfall, and its forest coverage ranks first in the country. In 221 B.C., Minzhong Prefecture was founded. Since then, Fujian appeared as an administrative region in Chinese territory. Fujian has been inhabited by various ethnic groups

• 福建武夷山茶园
Tea Plantation in Wuyi Mountain, Fujian Province

种客家文化的特点。精雕细琢的红砖白石、高大的封火墙、弯曲的屋脊、飞翘的檐角，再加上敦实厚重的客家土楼，每一处都蕴含着丰富的历史文化信息。

since old times. However, due to wars or natural disasters, a large number of Hakka migrated to the area, bringing unique culture to Fujian. The architecture of Fujian ancient towns fully embodies the characteristics of the Hakka culture. The richly ornamented red bricks and white stones, tall firewalls, curved roof ridges, upturned eaves, coupled with the solid and thick Hakka earthen buildings, are all permeated with a rich historical and cultural note.

• 浮雕八仙上寿图寿山石章（清）
Shoushan Stone Seal with Relief "The Eight Immortals Offering Birthday Congratulations" (Qing Dynasty 1616-1911)

长汀

长汀隶属福建省龙岩市，位于福建西部的汀江上游、武夷山脉南段，重峦叠嶂，是闽、粤、赣三省的边陲要冲。长汀的历史十分悠久。据考古发现，早在旧石器时代，这里就有人类活动，至新石器时代，古闽人在此繁衍生息。唐代开元二十四年（736年），置汀州，至今有近1300年的历史。两晋时期，大批中原士族为躲避战乱南迁到这里定居，成为最早的客家先

Changting

Part of Longyan City, Fujian Province, Changting is located in the upper reaches of the Tingjiang River and the southern section of Wuyi Mountains in western Fujian. Encircled by mountains, it is an important place at the junction of Fujian, Guangdong and Jiangxi provinces. Changting has a long history. According to archaeological discoveries, there were human activities as early as the Paleolithic Age; down to the Neolithic Age, the ancient clan of Min lived and multiplied here. In 736 of the Tang

- 长汀古城墙 (图片提供：FOTOE)
  Ancient City Wall of Changting

民。到宋代，汀州已经是客家人聚居的城镇，也是客家文化的发源地。

长汀古城墙始建于唐大历四年（769年），已有1200多年历史。初建时城墙为土筑，防御设施简单。明洪武四年（1371年），土城墙全部筑以砖石。现存的古城墙全长1500多米，以汀江为界向两边延伸至卧龙山顶，沿山脉蜿蜒而下将整个县城包围，犹如一串佛珠，被称为"佛挂珠"。

Dynasty, Tingzhou was founded. In the Western and Eastern Jin dynasties (265-420), people from the Central Plains came to the area in droves, fleeing wars and disasters, and they became the first Hakka ancestors. By the Song Dynasty (960-1279), Tingzhou has been a area inhabited by the Hakka people and the birthplace of the Hakka culture.

The ancient city wall was built of dirt in 769 of the Tang Dynasty with simple defense facilities; in 1371 of

客家人

客家人是从西晋时期起，由于战乱、饥荒等原因，中原的汉族人逐渐南下进入赣、闽、粤三角区，与当地畲族、瑶族等居民杂处，互通婚姻，发生融合而形成的一个独特而稳定的汉族支系。他们有独特的客家方言、生活习俗。福建省宁化县石壁是客家传说民系形成的中心地域，被称为"客家祖地"。而客家人聚居的惠州、梅州、赣州、汀州，被认为是客家大本营，称"客家四州"。近代以来繁衍扩展到台、港、澳地区及海外的后裔，也皆称客家人。

Hakka

The Hakka people are a unique subgroup of Han. Because of war, famine and other reasons, they have since the Western Jin Dynasty (265-317) migrated gradually to Jiangxi, Fujian and Guangdong Triangle Region, where they mixed with local ethnic groups such as She and Yao and exchanged marriage with each other. The Hakka people have their own language and cultural customs. Shibi Village of Ninghua County, Fujian Province, is the ancestral home of the Hakka people, while Huizhou, Meizhou, Ganzhou and Tingzhou, where the Hakka people live in compact communities, are considered their home base. In modern times, their descendants who migrated to Taiwan, Hong Kong, Macao regions of China and overseas countries are also called the Hakka people.

• 汀州试院内的参天唐柏（图片提供：FOTOE）
The Huge Cypress Trees in the Courtyard of Tingzhou Examination Center

the Ming Dynasty the entire earth wall was enclosed by bricks and stones. The ancient wall that survived today is over 1,500 meters in length. From the highest point on the Wolong (Reclining Dragon) Mountain the wall descends east and west toward the Tingjiang River at the foot of the mountain, wrapping all of Changting town within its embrace. Seen from the summit, the wall looks just like a string of prayer beads, known as *Foguazhu*.

The Tingzhou Examination Center is situated in Zhaozheng Road, Changting Old City. Built in the Song Dynasty (960-1279), the courtyard-style compound covers an area of more than 10,000 square meters, consisting of the gate tower, the courtyard, the main hall, the rear hall, wing rooms and several bungalows. In the Song Dynasty (960-1279), the compound was where the headquarters of Tingzhou household troops was located. It was designated to be an examination center in the Ming and Qing dynasties, holding county level examinations. In the courtyard two

长汀古城兆征路的汀州试院，始建于宋代，庭院式结构，占地万余平方米，由门楼、空坪、大堂、后厅、厢房和数幢平房组成。这里在宋代原为汀州禁军署地，明清时辟为试院，是古代汀州八县八邑科举秀才应试的场所。院内生长着两棵珍稀的唐代柏树，参天繁茂，是汀州古城的历史见证。

永定

永定位于福建省西南部的龙岩市，地处闽粤两省交界处的丘陵地区。永定历史悠久，在古代曾长期处于动乱中。明成化十四年（1478年）从上杭县分出置县，取名"永定"，意在"永远安定"。

被誉为"世界上独一无二的山村民居建筑"的永定客家土楼，因奇特的建筑艺术和丰富的客家文化内涵而备受瞩目。土楼俗称"生土楼"，因大多数为福建客家人所建，故又称"客家土楼"，是以生土作为主要建筑材料，生土掺上细

lush cypress trees rise high into the sky; planted in the Tang Dynasty (618-907), they are the historical testimony of the ancient city of Tingzhou.

Yongding

Yongding is a part of Longyan City in the southwest of Fujian Province; it is a hilly area located at the junction of Fujian and Guangdong provinces. The age-old Yongding was plagued by unrest for a long period in old times. In 1478 Zhixian County was separated from Hangxian

- 永定土楼集庆楼鸟瞰
  Overlooking the Jiqing House—the *Tulou* of Yongding

振成楼外观

客家土楼有圆楼与方楼之分，振成楼是典型的圆形土楼，又称"圆寨"。

Appearance of Zhencheng House

Hakka *Tulou* contain round ones and rectangular ones. Zhencheng House is a typical round building, also known as "Round Village".

沙、石灰、糯米饭、红糖、竹片、木条等，经过反复揉、舂、压后，用于建造。楼顶覆以火烧瓦盖，经久不损。土楼高可达四五层，供三代或四代人同楼聚居。

振成楼是客家土楼中的精品，建于1912年。振成楼的设计十分独特，采用了中国传统的八卦图结构，因此俗称"八卦楼"。整个土楼规模宏大，占地约5000平方米，费时5年才建成。

振成楼分内外两圈，形成"楼中有楼"的格局。外楼圈4层，每层48间，按照中国传统的八卦图分为放射状的8个单元（卦），每

County, and was named "Yongding", which implies "stable forever".

Tulou of Yongding attracts wide attention with its unusual architectural art and rich connotations of Hakka culture; it is reputed as "The residential building that is unique in the world". *Tulou*, commonly known as "*Sheng Tulou*" (rammed-earth building), is also called "Hakka *Tulou*" because they are mostly built by the Hakka people in Fujian Province. Such houses are constructed of the mixture of raw soil, fine sand, lime, glutinous rice, brown sugar, bamboo, wood, etc.; the roofs are covered with specially fired tiles that are solid and durable. About four or five stories tall,

● 振成楼内西洋风格的祖堂

土楼中的祖堂是土楼客家人聚族而居的重要证明，它通常位于全楼的核心位置，既是全楼居民祭祀祖宗的场所，又是进行社交活动的中心。一般祖堂内正中墙上设有神座，两边墙上挂祖宗画像，下面摆设供桌。

The Western-style Ancestral Hall of Zhencheng House

The ancestral hall of *Tulou* provides an important proof that the Hakka people live in a compact community. Located usually in the central position of the house, it is where all the residents in the compound worship the ancestors and hold social activities. In the hall, a shrine is often placed in the middle section of the wall, and the portraits of the ancestors are hung on side walls; under the portraits are the altars.

"卦"6间，设一楼梯，"卦"与"卦"之间以拱门相通。相邻的两"卦"之间有青砖砌筑的隔火墙，一"卦"失火，不会殃及全楼。"卦"与"卦"之间还设"卦门"，关闭起来自成一个院落，开启后可贯通全楼。楼内正中有祖堂，就像一个舞台，两侧上下两层

they can accommodate large families with three or four generations.

Built in 1912, Zhencheng House is the representative of Hakka *Tulou*. It adopts an unusual design—the structure of traditional Chinese Eight Diagrams—and is commonly known as "The House of Eight Diagrams". The huge compound occupies an area of about 5,000 square

圈成一个内圈，用砖木仿西洋式装修，形成"外土内洋，中西合璧"的独特风格。楼内有众多名流名家楹联，充分展示了土楼的文化内涵。主楼左右两侧还分别建有学堂和其他附属建筑。

承启楼从明崇祯年间（1628—1644）破土奠基，到清康熙四十八年（1709年）竣工，经过建造者江氏家族三代人的不懈努力，方才建成这座巨大的家族之城。承启楼全楼直径73米，外墙周长1915米，走廊周长229.34米，结构为"三圈一中心"。外圈四层，每层72个房间；

meters and took five years to build.

Zhencheng House contains two concentric rings, a pattern that shows buildings encircling buildings. The outer ring has four stories; the 48 rooms on each floor are divided into eight units (*Gua*) in accordance with traditional Chinese Eight Diagrams, each unit having 6 rooms and a staircase. All units are connected to each other with arched doors; a firewall made of gray bricks is built between two neighboring units, to prevent fire from spreading into other parts of the house. Between them there is also a door, closed to form an individual courtyard and opened to make a passage

- **承启楼第一层的回廊**
  一层主要是厨房，因靠近水井，方便取水和洗涤。
  Corridor on the Ground Floor of Chengqi House
  The ground floor is mainly reserved for kitchen because it is convenient to get water from the wells nearby.

第二圈有两层，每层40个房间；第三圈为单层，32个房间，中心为祖堂。全楼共有400个房间，3个大门，两口水井，整个建筑占地面积5376.17平方米。鼎盛时期承启楼里同时住过800多人，就像一个热闹的小城市。由于规模宏大，承启楼有"土楼之王"的美誉。

遗经楼建于清咸丰元年（1851年），是永定土楼中规模较大的方楼之一。外墙东西宽136米，南北长76米，占地10336平方米，楼内共有房间267间，51个大小厅堂。主楼左右两端分别垂直连着一座四层

• 遗经楼平面示意图
Plan Sketch of Yijing House

through the entire house. The innermost building is used as the ancestral hall, which appears as a stage encircled by two-storied wings on both sides. The hall is built of brick and wood with Western-style decoration, delivering a distinctive style that combines Chinese and Western elements. In the hall are hung many couplets dedicated by celebrities and distinguished personages, which fully demonstrates the artistic appeal of *Tulou*. Flanking the ancestral hall stand a school and other outbuildings.

The construction of Chengqi House started between 1628 and 1644, and was completed in 1709. It took the Jiang family over 80 years of efforts to build this huge compound. The house has four concentric rings, with a diameter of 73 meters, the circumference of the external wall and corridor being 1,915 meters and 229.34 meters respectively. The outer ring is four-storied, with 72 rooms on each floor; the second ring has two stories, each having 40 rooms; the single-story third ring has 32 rooms and encircles an ancestral hall at the center. The whole compound has 400 rooms, three doors and two wells, covering an area of 5,376.17 square meters. In its heyday, this massive building was just like a

• 遗经楼内大门
Inner Gate of Yijing House

的楼房，并与主楼平行的四层前楼紧紧相接，围成一个巨大的方楼，环绕形成一个大"口"字形，里面又有一组小的"口"字形建筑，形成独特的"回"字形结构，当地人称它为"大楼厦"。前楼一左一右建有两所学堂，楼内子女可以在楼内就读。整个建筑布局规整，条理井然，当地人用夸张的语言形容其大：一个人从太阳升起即开始开窗，开到中午下楼吃饭，然后上楼关窗，直到太阳下山才关完最后一扇窗。

bustling small city, holding over 800 people. Owing much to its scale, Chengqi House earns itself the accolade "King of *Tulou*".

Yijing House, built in 1851, is among the largest rectangular earthen houses of Yongding. The external wall is 136 meters wide from east to west and 76 meters long from north to south, covering an area of 10,336 square meters; the compound has 267 rooms and 51 halls of various sizes. The right and left ends of the main building are attached respectively at right angle to two four-story buildings, which connect seamlessly

广西古镇

广西地处中国南部，属亚热带季风气候区，夏天时间长、气温较高、降水多，冬天时间短、天气干。广西历史悠久，在旧石器时代晚期就有远古先民在此劳作生息。

桂北地区是广西古镇保存最多的地方。这些古镇多为明清时期所建，既受中原传统文化的影响，

桂林漓江风光
Scenery of Lijiang River, Guilin

with another four-story construction that sits parallel to the main building, forming a huge square building that shapes like the Chinese character "口". Encircled by this one is a smaller square construction. Seen from above, the whole compound looks like the Chinese character "回", and the locals call it "*Dalousha*" (grand building). To the left and right of the front building are two annexes, where the children in the compound attend school. The whole compound is neatly and orderly laid out. Its vastness is described by locals as "This huge compound has so many windows that one would have to spend a whole day opening and closing them once each".

Guangxi Ancient Towns

Located in southern China, Guangxi has a subtropical monsoon climate; summers are long and hot, with abundant rainfall, while winters are short, dry and warm. Guangxi has a long history. As early as the late Paleolithic Age there were people living in this place.

Northern Guangxi boasts the largest number of ancient towns in the province. These ancient towns were mostly built in the Ming and Qing dynasties; they display a blend of traditional culture from

也有广西地方特色。桂西地区在古时少有人居住，后来逐渐发展成为少数民族的聚居地。高山上、江水旁成了苗、瑶、侗、壮等少数民族栖身的家园，吊脚楼、风雨桥、鼓楼等独具特色的建筑散布在大山之间，具有浓郁的少数民族风情。而桂东南地区处于两广交界处，融合了广东、广西的文化，水运交通相当发达，历史上就是商贾云集之地。广西作为明清时期对外贸易的口岸，又临近曾是法属殖民地的越南，所以现存古镇大都受到欧洲建筑风格影响，民居多为砖砌的骑楼。

黄姚

黄姚镇位于广西贺州昭平县东北部，是有着近千年历史的古镇，发祥于宋朝，兴建于明朝万历年间（1573—1620），鼎盛于清朝乾隆年间（1736—1795）。由于镇上以黄、姚两姓居多，故名"黄姚镇"。

黄姚古镇街道全部用青色石板镶嵌而成，路面平滑如镜。镇内的建筑按九宫八卦阵势布局，属岭南风格建筑，与周围环境形成一体，

the Central Plains and the local features of Guangxi. Western Guangxi, where few people lived in ancient times, later evolved into a gathering place of some ethnic groups such as Zhuang, Miao, Yao and Dong. These ethnic groups dwell in the mountains and along the rivers; their hanging houses, wind and rain bridges, and drum towers scatter in the mountains and exhibit an exotic and enchanting flavor. Bordered by Guangdong, eastern and southern Guangxi has a hybrid culture of both provinces and well-developed water transportation, and has been a commercial center since old times. In the Ming and Qing dynasties it used to be a foreign trade zone sitting near Vietnam—a former French colony, so the existing old towns are mostly influenced by the European architectural style, and the residential houses are mainly arcade buildings built of bricks.

Huangyao

Located northeast of Zhaoping County, Hezhou City, Huangyao is an old town with a thousand years of history. It originated in the Song Dynasty, was established in the Ming Dynasty and flourished in the Qianlong Period of the Qing Dynasty. The family names of the townspeople were mainly Huang

是一个天然的山水园林古镇。现在古镇完整保存着明清古建筑300多幢，房屋多为两层的砖瓦结构，建筑精美，砖雕、石雕、木雕都有很高的工艺水平。古建筑的梁柱、斗拱、檩椽、墙面、天花都精心雕饰，图案千姿百态。另外，黄姚镇还有景观建筑亭台楼阁10多处，寺观庙祠20多座，特色桥梁11座，楹联匾额上百副。

黄姚古镇素有"梦境家园"之称。镇内山水岩洞多，亭台楼阁多，寺观多，祠堂多，古树多，楹联匾额多。有山必有水，有水必有桥，有桥必有亭，有亭必有联，有

• 黄姚古镇的千年古榕 (图片提供：FOTOE)
Old Banyan Tree, Huangyao

and Yao, so the place became known as Huangyao Town.

The ancient streets of Huangyao are all paved by flagstones that are smooth like mirrors. The town's architectures, planned according to the Eight-diagram Formation, are of southland style and well integrated with nature, creating a natural landscape garden. Today it has over 300 well-preserved buildings of Ming and Qing dynasties, most of which are of two-story brick and tile structure, with exquisite brick, stone and wood carvings; the beams, brackets, purlins, rafters, walls and ceilings of these buildings are all richly ornamented and display diversified patterns. The town also houses 20-plus temples and ancestral halls, 10-plus pavilions, 11 unique bridges, as well as numerous plaques, couplets and scrolls.

Reputed as "Dream Home", the old town of Huangyao enjoys a large number of landscapes and grottos, pavilions, temples and ancestral halls, old trees, couplets and plaques. Mountains, water, bridges, pavilions, along with the couplets and plaques, create a unique scene in perfect harmony.

In many ancient towns, the prominent families have their own ancestral halls, and Huangyao is no exception. Among

● 带龙桥 (图片提供：FOTOE)
Dailong Bridge

联必有匾，构成古镇独特的风景。

　　同许多古镇一样，当地旺族大姓必有一座祠堂，黄姚也少不了祠堂。黄姚至今仍完好保留着明清时期的十余座宗祠，其中以古氏、莫氏和劳氏宗祠规模最大。各宗祠每年都有独特的祭祖活动，不同的姓氏在不同的时间举行。黄姚的宗祠建筑结构精致，装饰豪华，门前有大石阶，祠内有宽阔的门廊，正中还有天井，两旁有小花园，独具桂北屋宇风格。墙上刻有花鸟壁画，

the 10-plus well-preserved ancestral halls of the Ming and Qing dynasties, the Gu, Mo and Lao families' ancestral halls are the largest. Each year these ancestral halls will hold worship activities in their own ways, different times being designated for different families. Huangyao's ancestral halls are of the architectural style of northern Guangxi, featuring exquisite structures and a magnificent decoration: massive stone steps lead up to the gate, inside which is a wide porch; in the center of the hall there is an atrium, flanked by small gardens; on the walls

这些壁画构图美观，工艺精湛，风格独特。

古戏台始建于明万历初年，至今已有400多年的历史。这座戏台属于亭阁式建筑，以8根木柱作支架，平面呈"凸"字形。戏台雕梁画栋，古朴典雅，阁顶塑有二龙戏珠。前台天花板中间有一幅"双凤奔月图"，色彩绚丽，富有民族艺术特色。戏台底部四周用方形大石

are carved murals depicting flowers and birds, which show well-balanced composition, exquisite workmanship and unique style.

Dating back to the early years of Wanli Period of the Ming Dynasty, the ancient opera stage has a history of over 400 years. A pavilion-style building supported by eight wooden columns, the stage is in the shape of the Chinese character "凸". This simple and elegant

- 黄姚古镇梁氏宗祠 (图片提供：FOTOE)
  The Liang's Ancestral Hall, Huangyao

● 黄姚古镇的古戏台 （图片提供：FOTOE）
Ancient Opera Stage, Huangyao

板围砌，牢固美观。前台地面铺设火砖，再铺设木板，与地面架空，形成共鸣。旧时台底四角还放置大水缸，以增强共鸣效果，所以每当台上锣鼓齐鸣时，10公里外的高地都可听到唱戏的声音。

大圩

大圩古镇位于桂林市东南18公里处，地处漓江中游北岸。大圩古镇始建于北宋初年，中兴于明清，鼎盛于民国时期，距今已有千年历史。作为水陆交通枢纽，大圩镇在北宋时已经是商业繁华的集镇，明清时更为发达，云集在此的商人陆续在此修建会馆。到民国初期，大

stage is richly ornamented, with a sculpture of "two dragons playing with a pearl" on its top. The ceiling above the stage is painted with a picture depicting two phoenixes flying to the moon, the picture being vibrantly colored and of rich ethnic features. The four sides of the stage foundation are surfaced with square stone slabs, a structure that is both solid and beautiful. The ground of the stage is paved by bricks, on which are placed wooden planks to create a resonant cavity. In old times, there used to be large water vats placed in the four corners underneath the stage to enhance reverberation, so whenever drums and gongs are blaring on the stage, the sound could be heard 10 kilometers away.

Daxu

The old town of Daxu is located 18 kilometers southeast of Guilin City, on the north bank of middle reaches of the Lijiang River. Dating back more than a thousand years, the town was built in the early years of the Northern Song Dynasty, prospered in the Ming and Qing dynasties and flourished in the Minguo Period. As a land and water transportation hub, Daxu had been a commercial center in the Northern Song Dynasty,

圩镇上已形成8条大街，沿江一带的码头也更加繁忙。大圩老街顺着漓江绵延两公里，不宽的街道上铺着青石板，石板路旁的房子多为青砖、青瓦的两层明清建筑，历史沧桑随处可见。镇中的民居建筑南低北高，临江依山而建，多为三进、四进式院落，集商、住于一体，均由门前、天井、正房、厢房、后院

大圩古镇的老街 (图片提供：FOTOE)
Ancient Street, Daxu

and down to the Ming and Qing it was much more developed, and merchants that gathered here started to construct guild halls. Towards the early years of the Minguo Period, there were 8 main streets in the town and the ports were busier than ever. The old street of Daxu runs two kilometers along the Lijiang River; along the narrow flagstone-paved street are two-story houses of the Ming and Qing dynasties built of gray bricks and tiles. The vicissitudes of history can be seen everywhere. The town was constructed fronting the river and with mountains at its back; the residential buildings, undulating following the rise and fall of the terrain, are mostly compounds with three or four successive courtyards; these buildings include shops and living quarters in one compound, and they consist of the front courtyard, atrium, main rooms, wing rooms and the rear courtyard; doors and windows of main and wing rooms are all carved with patterns. A number of ancient workshops still exist in the town, including bamboo-weaving workshops, sandal workshops, stores that sell traditional funeral goods, a herbal medicine clinic, and an old barber shop.

Wanshou Bridge or the Bridge of

组成。正房、厢房的门窗上都雕有花纹。古镇现在还保留着许多竹编作坊、草鞋作坊、传统的丧葬用品店、草医诊室、老理发店等一批古老的作坊。

万寿桥位于马河与漓江汇合处，始建于明代，最初为木结构的三拱板桥，后毁于水灾，于清光绪二十八年（1902年）重建为单拱石桥。桥全长29.6米，高7.1米，净跨16.8米，两边各有二十余级台阶，桥面以青石板嵌成，两侧有护栏，总体造型稳健古朴。桥面的石头历经百年已被磨得溜光发亮，间杂些许小草，显得古朴自然。

Longevity, built in the Ming Dynasty, lies where the Mahe River and the Lijiang River meet. It was originally a three-arch wooden bridge, and was later destroyed by flood. The present single-arch stone bridge is a reconstruction in 1902. The bridge is 29.6 meters long and 7.1 meters high, with a span of 16.8 meters. At both ends of the bridge are 20-plus steps leading up respectively to thebridge deck, which is paved by flagstones and flanked by balustrades. The bridge looks firm and quaint; its stones on the bridge deck, after a hundred years' wear-out, become smooth and shiny. In stone crevices there grows some grass, lending the bridge a simple and natural note.

> 西南古镇

西南各省区自古以来就是多民族混居的地区，所以此区域内的古镇古村建筑各有其民族特色，如傣族的干栏式建筑、苗族的吊脚楼等，具有很浓的民族风情。

四川古镇

四川省简称"川"或"蜀"，位于中国西南地区、长江上游。川西为高原，其余为四川盆地。其中居住着彝族、藏族、回族、汉族、羌族等民族。四川的古镇主要集中在东部和南部，依山傍水，而且多在古代交通要道周围，建筑风格兼具粗犷与灵巧，体现了巴蜀文化的精髓。

> Ancient Towns in Southwest China

Since old times, the southwestern provinces and regions have been the region where various ethnic groups inhabit. Towns and villages in this area have their own characteristics, such as pile-dwellings of Dai, and stilted houses of Miao.

Sichuan Ancient Towns

Sichuan Province, called "Chuan" or "Shu" for short, is located southwest of China, in the upper reaches of the Yangtze River. Consisting of plateau area in the western part and basin in its east, Sichuan is inhabited by Yi people, Zang people, Hui people, Han people, and Qiang people, etc. Ancient towns

四川川西风光
Scenery of Western Sichuan

黄龙溪

黄龙溪古镇位于成都市双流区内，至今已有1700余年的历史，历来就是成都南面的军事重镇。黄龙溪东临府河，北靠牧马山，旧时水运交通十分发达，外来商客很多，航运上达成都，下通重庆，是水路运输的重要码头。这里依山傍水，风景秀丽，现存的民居多为明清时期的建筑。主街道由石板铺就，两旁是飞檐翘角干栏式吊脚

of Sichuan are mainly concentrated in the eastern and southern part of the province, where they are encircled by rivers and mountains and are mostly located along the ancient traffic arteries. Their architectural style is both rustic and delicate, a trait that embodies the essence of the Ba-Shu culture.

Huanglongxi

Huanglongxi, an old town with over 1,700 years of history, is located in Shuangliu County, Chengdu City.

• 黄龙溪的吊脚楼

黄龙溪古镇内，顺河而建的吊脚楼比比皆是。这些吊脚楼多为木结构，飞檐翘角，古意十足。

Stilted Houses, Huanglongxi

In Huanglongxi, Hanging houses can be seen everywhere along the river. Such houses are mostly of wooden structure with upswept eaves, lending the town a quaint atmosphere.

• 古镇特产的草鞋
Straw Sandals—Speciality of the Town

楼，一家挨一家。楼下临街都是店铺，乌黑发亮的门板，古色古香的招牌，透着浓浓古意。二楼的房子靠近内街的用作住宅，靠近河边的用来做生意。古民居、古牌坊、古寺庙、古榕树浑然一体。

古龙寺是黄龙溪修建最早的

It has historically been a military stronghold south of Chengdu. Sitting east of the Fuhe River and north of Muma Mountain, Huanglongxi used to be a main port linking Chengdu with Chongqing; its well-developed water transportation greatly facilitated passenger and freight transport. The town, fronting water and with a hill at the back, is suffused with natural beauty. Its existing residential buildings are mostly constructed in the Ming and Qing dynasties. The flagstone paved main street is thickly lined with stilted houses with upswept eaves; looking on the street, the rooms downstairs serve as shops where the glossy black-painted

寺庙，以古寺庙、古戏台、古榕树"三古"著称。古龙寺的古戏台名为"万年台"，建于清初，距今已有三百多年历史，是黄龙溪九个古戏台中仅存的一个。万年台院坝南北各有一棵古榕树，据考均已有

doors and the antique shop signs exude an air of antiquity. On the upper floor, rooms fronting the street are used as living quarters and those facing the river are reserved for business purposes. Ancient houses, archways, temples, and banyan trees form a successful combination of natural and cultural landscapes.

The oldest temple in Huanglongxi, Gulong Temple is known for the ancient temple, the opera stage and the banyan trees. Above the main entrance of the temple is an opera stage built in the early Qing Dynasty, named as Wannian Stage; with over 300 hundred years of history, it is the only existant among the nine ancient stages of Huanglongxi. The stage stands overlooking to an open ground, in south and north of which there is an ancient banyan tree respectively. The trees, said to have been over 900 years old, fit in well with the ancient temple. Opposite the stage is the Hall of Maitreya, in front of which stands an iron pagoda. Aside from the Hall of Maitreya, main buildings in Gulong Temple include the Avalokitesvara Hall, the halls of Avalokitesvara and Amitabha.

- 古龙寺
  Gulong Temple

900多年历史。万年台正对面是弥勒殿，弥勒殿前，矗立着一座千佛塔。除弥勒殿外，古龙寺现有的主要建筑还有大雄宝殿、观音堂和弥陀殿。

上里

上里镇位于四川省雅安市的北部，是四川历史文化名镇。上里古镇以前名叫"罗绳"，是历

Shangli

Shangli, situated in the northern part of Ya'an City, Sichuan Province, is a historical and cultural town of the province. Formerly known as Luosheng, Shangli used to be a key staging post on the route between the Southern Silk Road and Ya'an, and an important pass via which the tea leaves of Sichuan was transported to the area inhabited by Zang ethnic group; it was also the place where

• 上里古镇的古院落 (图片提供: FOTOE)
Ancient Courtyards, Shangli

史上南方丝绸之路进入雅安的重要驿站，也是将四川茶叶输入藏区茶道的重要关隘，历代茶马司（古代专门负责收购茶叶进贡皇室及管理汉藏茶马互换交易的机构）所在地。

古镇民居保存得基本完好，多为青瓦民居，高低错落，风格各异。街市主要是"井"字布局，取"井中有水"防止火患之意。从古镇沿河上溯一公里，共有十余座古桥，造型各异，这些桥梁不仅是南来北往的通道，还再现了古镇历史和造桥匠师的技艺。

二仙桥位于古镇西约200米处的陇西河上，最初建于清乾隆年间（1736—1795），曾两次被洪水冲毁，第三次重建于乾隆四十一年（1776年）。该桥为高卷拱单孔石桥，桥面两侧有石栏，正中雕刻龙头、龙尾，正面浮雕神像和"二仙桥"三个大字。二仙桥得名于一段神奇的传说，相传石桥建造之前，人们赶集只能分别在河的两岸，极不方便。有一天，有两个乞丐从人群中跳进江里，转眼就变成了两个石墩，人们就在石墩的基础上修建

Chamasi (A government office in charge of affairs relating to tea) of various dynasties was located.

Residential buildings of the town are mostly well-preserved. Houses tiles huddle in clusters, forming a roofscape like a rolling sea of blue tiles when seen from afar. Streets are planned in the shape of the Chinese character "井" (water well). This is symbolic in the sense that water from the well will quench fires. Up the river, about one kilometer away from the old town, there lie over 10 ancient bridges of various shapes, which not only serve as passages, but also represent the history of the ancient town and the skills of bridge-building craftsmen.

Lying over the Longxi River about 200 meters west of the town, Erxian Bridge was originally built in the Qianlong Period of the Qing Dynasty. It had been destroyed twice by floods, and the present bridge was a reconstruction in 1776. The bridge is of high-arch type with one curvature; on stone railings of the bridge are carved a dragon head and a tail as well as figures of various Gods in relief and three Chinese characters "Er Xian Qiao" (Erxian Bridge). This bridge took its name from a legend. The story goes that before the construction

长满藤蔓的二仙桥 (图片提供：FOTOE)
如今，古老的二仙桥桥身上已经爬满了藤蔓植物，却依然横跨在河上岿然不动，发挥着连接南北交通的作用。

Erxian Bridge Covered with Vines
The bridge, now covered with vines, is still sturdy and links the villages on both sides of the river.

了这座桥。后来人们认为这两个乞丐是仙人化身的，于是称这座桥为"二仙桥"。

双节孝牌坊位于古镇南四家村昔日的古道上，建于清道光十九年（1839年），是清廷为褒扬当地韩家婆媳二人守节而敕建的旌表节孝牌坊。坊上横额镌刻"双节孝"三字，脊顶下正中有"圣旨"二字。

of the bridge country fairs had to be held respectively on both sides of the river, which was inconvenient. One day, two beggars jumped into the river, and quickly turned into two piers. Based on these piers, locals constructed the bridge. The two beggars were thus thought to be the incarnation of immortals, hence the name "Erxian" (two immortals).

The Memorial Archway of Chastity

牌坊采用当地优质石英红砂岩石建造，通高11.25米，进深3米。牌坊上雕刻的图案内容非常丰富，多为镂空或半镂空的深浮雕，雕刻技艺十分精湛。共有浮雕169幅，圆雕13座，雕刻人物571个，内容以戏曲题材为多，也有部分出自小说、传说故事等，都以"忠、孝、节、义"为主题。

and Filial Piety, located in the former ancient road of the town, was built in 1839 at the behest of Qing imperial court in honor of the mother-in-law and daughter-in-law of the Han family who never remarried after their husbands' death. In the horizontal tablet of the archway are engraved three Chinese characters "*Shuang Jie Xiao*" (Chastity and Filial Piety of Two Women); right below the rooftop are carved the characters "*Sheng Zhi*" (Imperial Edict). The archway is built of local-quarried top grade red quartz rock, with a height of 11.25 meters and a depth of 3 meters. The carvings on the archway feature rich and varied motifs, mostly executed in high relief; the carving skills are superb, as best seen on 169 reliefs, 13 round carvings, and 571 carved figures. The subject matters are chiefly taken from operas, novels, legends, etc., with "Loyalty, Filial piety, Chastity and Integrity" being always the motif.

• 双节孝牌坊 (图片提供：FOTOE)
Memorial Archway of Chastity and Filial Piety

云南古镇

　　云南简称"云"或"滇"，地处中国西南边陲。云南现有的十余座古镇，大都建于古大理国时期，分布在云南各地。这些古镇在历史上都是当地的经济文化中心，所以留下了浓厚的经济特色，同时具有浓郁的少数民族风情。其中大理

• 云南香格里拉风光

Yunnan Ancient Towns

Yunnan, abbreviated as "Yun" or "Dian" is located in the far southwest of China. A dozen extant old towns in Yunnan were mostly established in the period of Dali Kingdom and are distributed throughout the province. Historically, these towns were the economic and cultural centers in their respective

Scenery of Shangrila Region, Yunnan Province

白族民居以"三坊一照壁""四合五天井"的布局而著称,粉墙黛瓦的院落无论是木雕、施彩、石刻还是泥工都丝毫不逊于江南园林与北方大宅。而干栏式竹楼是云南南部傣、佤、苗等少数民族的主要民居形式。滇南气候炎热,潮湿多雨,竹楼下部架空,可通风隔潮;上层前部有宽廊和晒台,后部为堂屋和卧室,屋顶出檐深远,可遮阳挡雨。

丽江

丽江古城位于云南省丽江纳西族自治县,地处青藏高原南端山峰耸峙的横断山脉,东与四川毗邻,北同西藏接壤,是云南通往西藏的必经之地。早在南宋时期,丽江古城就已初具规模,至今已有八九百年的历史。清代,随着茶马贸易的日渐繁荣,丽江的商贸市场已有相当规模,并成为货物到藏区的商贸中转站以及来往马帮、客商歇脚和打尖的地方。

丽江是一个纳西、汉族、白族、傈僳族、彝族、苗族等多民族杂居的地方,丰富多样的文化习俗、生活方式和多种语言通用,来

regions, hence they are known for their economic characteristics as well as the rich ethnic customs. The residential buildings of the Bai people are the representative of the many kinds of architecture in Dali. These courtyard buildings of the Bai people are partly similar to those of Beijing in North China: (1) there is usually a screen wall set between the yard and the main gate; (2) the screen wall is replaced by a building, which joins the buildings on the other three sides to form an enclosed compound. Exquisite carvings, paintings and other decorations found on these buildings are in no way inferior to those in gardens of Jiangnan region and large mansions in North China. Bamboo pile-dwellings are common in the southern Yunnan, where Dai, Wa, Miao and other ethnic groups reside. To adapt to the hot, humid and rainy weather, the bamboo houses are raised on stilts above ground to create a space underneath the house for ventilation and moisture insulation; in the upper front of the house is a veranda; the upper rear part serves as living room and bedroom with projecting eaves for keeping out burning sun and rain.

Lijiang

Part of Lijiang Naxi Autonomous County,

丽江古城的石板街道
Flagstone-paved Streets, Lijiang

自山南海北的商家都感到方便，再加上四季宜人的气候，很多内地商人到丽江就驻足不前，将此地作为经营生意的基地。

丽江民谚说："先有四方街，后有丽江城。"四方街是古城的中心，丽江古城就是以四方街为基础发展起来的。四方街当年由土司取名，取"权镇四方"之意。也有人说是因为这里的道路通向四面八方，是四面八方的人流、物流集散地，所以叫"四方街"。

Yunnan Province, the old town of Lijiang is located at the foot of Hengduan Mountains in the southern end of the Qinghai-Xizang Plateau. Bordering Sichuan Province in the east and Xizang to the north, it is the only passage linking Yunnan and Xizang. As early as in the Southern Song Dynasty (1127-1279), Lijiang began to take shape. In the Qing Dynasty (1616-1911) when trade was growing steadily, the commerce market in Lijiang has been of considerable size; the town became a transit station via

古往今来，四方街都是藏区及丽江的马匹、毛皮、藏药等特产和南方的茶叶、丝绸、珠宝等商品的贸易中心。白天，这里商贾云集，买卖兴隆；中午前后，会有许多身穿传统服装的纳西族老人伴着古老的乐曲跳起民族舞蹈；到了夜晚，特别是节日的夜晚，各族民众来到这里燃起篝火，唱

which goods were transported to the area inhabited by Zang ethnic group, and where traveling merchants and horse caravans stopped for refreshment.

Lijiang is inhabited by Naxi, Han, Bai, Lisu, Yi, Miao and other ethnic groups. Owing much to its rich and diverse cultural practices, lifestyles, languages and the pleasant climate, Lijiang was favored by businessmen from across

- 玉龙雪山下的丽江古城
  The Old Town of Lijiang at the Foot of Yulong Snow Mountain

起山歌，跳起民族舞蹈，通宵达旦地狂欢。

明代末年，丽江日渐繁荣，木氏土司所营造的土司府非常华美，明代旅行家徐霞客在游记中称其"宫室之丽，拟于王者"。木府占地46亩，整个建筑群坐西朝东，分别有议事厅、万卷楼、护法殿等大殿，两侧房屋罗列。花园回廊，楼台亭阁，数不胜数，风格别致。木府建筑在明代中原建筑风格基础上，融入了纳西族和白族的地方风格，同时将云南名木古树、奇花异

• 在四方街跳起民族舞蹈的纳西族人和游客
Dancing Naxis and Vtsitors in Sifang Street

the country. Many of them settled and opened businesses here.

Sifang Street is the center of the old town, and the latter was developed based on this street. As the saying goes, "Sifang Street appeared ahead of Lijiang". Sifang, which means "Power is everywhere", or literally "four directions", was named by aboriginal official. Some believe it was so named because streets and lanes radiate out from Sifang Street, where people and goods from all quarters converge.

Throughout the ages, Sifang Street was the trade center of Lijiang and areas inhabited by Zang ethnic group, the commodity involving horses, fur, Tibetan medicine and other specialties as well as tea, silk, jewelry from southern China. During the day, the street was crowded with merchants and businesses were brisk; around noon, many old Naxi people in traditional clothes would perform their folk dance to the ancient music. When night fell, people of all ethnic groups came here, lighting the bonfire, singing folk songs, performing folk dance and raving all night long.

Towards the end of the Ming dynasty, Lijiang witnessed its heyday. Aboriginal Official Mu's Mansion, as the traveler and writer Xu Xiake of the

● 丽江木氏土司府

木氏土司历经元、明、清三代，22世470年，以"知诗书好礼守义"而著称。

Tusi (Aboriginal Official) Mu's Mansion, Lijiang
The Mu family, survived right through the Ming and Qing dynasties. Over several centuries, the Tusi title was passed down 22 generations of the Mu family, who were noted for their erudition, propriety and righteousness.

草汇聚一所，将自然清雅之气与土司王宫的典雅富丽融为一体，充分展现了丽江文化的开放精神。

大理

大理古城又称"榆城"，始建于公元1382年，素有"文献名邦"之称，是云南最早的文化发祥地之一。这里气候温和，土地肥沃，风

Ming Dynasty described, was no inferior in size or lavishness to royal residence. The compound, built facing east, consists of a great many buildings, covering an area of more than 3 hectares; the houses, gardens, corridors and pavilions in the compound were unique and elegant. These Ming-style buildings display a blend of architectural style of heartland China and the local flavor of Naxi

光秀丽，有下关风、上关花、苍山雪、洱海月等美景，因而有"风花雪月"的美称。远在4000多年前，大理地区就有原始居民生活。唐代初年，洱海地区"六诏"（唐初分布在洱海地区的六大少数民族部落）中的蒙舍诏势力渐强，在唐朝的支持下，于开元二十六年（738年）统一"六诏"，建立了南诏国。南诏时期，大理地区的政治、经济、文化、生产技术都有了长足的发展，享誉海内外的崇圣寺三塔就是当时的产物。

现在的大理古城始建于明洪武十五年（1382年），方圆十二里，东西南北各设一门，均有城楼，四角还有角楼。由南门进城，一条直通北门的复兴路，成了繁华的街市，沿街店铺比肩而设，出售各种民族工艺品及珠宝玉石。街巷保存着不少明清时期的民居老宅。传统上大理每户人家都有花园，栽种著名的大理山茶花、杜鹃花，各种花伸出墙外，争奇斗艳，花香四时不绝；还有泉水从城外苍山流进城里，经过每家门前，大街小巷水声不绝。"家家流水，户户养花"名不虚传。

and Bai ethnic groups. Moreover, the compound has a rich collection of exotic flowers and herbs, rare plants of various kinds, which amass natural elegance and royal magnificence in perfect harmony and fully demonstrate the openness of the Lijiang culture.

Dali

The old town of Dali was constructed in 1382; it is a place famous for many informative local chronicles and is one of the earliest birthplaces of culture in Yunnan. Dali is blessed with mild climate, fertile land and beautiful scenery. Locals summarize their natural attractions as "wind, flowers, snow and moon", referring respectively to the seasonal wind in Xiaguan, the blossom of woodlotus trees in Shangguan, the snowscapes of Cangshan Mountain and the night view of Erhai Lake. As far back as 4,000 years ago, Dali was inhabited by early tribal men. In the early years of the Tang Dynasty (618-907), there used to be six minority tribes in Erhai area, which was later unified by one of the tribes with the support of the Tang Dynasty. In 738, Nanzhao Kingdom was established. During the Nanzhao Period, politics, economy, culture and production technology of Dali region had developed

大理背靠苍山，面临洱海。苍山，又名"点苍山"，主要由19座山峰组成，最高峰海拔4000多米，其他山峰海拔也都在3500米以上。苍山景色向来以雪、云、泉著称。经夏不消的苍山雪，是素负盛名的大理"风花雪月"四景之最。在苍山顶上，有很多高山冰碛湖泊，湖泊四周是遮天蔽日的原始森林。18条溪水倾泻于19峰之间，点缀了苍山风光。洱海是一个风光明媚的高

by leaps and bounds, and the well-known Three Pagodas of Dali were constructed in this period.

Built in 1382, the present town of Dali occupies an area of several square kilometers. The town is walled on four sides, each having a gate and gate tower; on the four corners there are turrets. Fuxing Road, bisecting the town from north to south, is packed with all kinds of shops selling ethnic handicrafts and jewelry. Well-preserved buildings dating to Ming and Qing dynasties can still be seen in streets and lanes of the old town. In most family's yards, there is a garden, where camellia and

正在制作扎染布的白族女子

扎染是白族人的传统民间工艺，原料为棉麻质地的白布，染料为苍山上生长的蓼蓝、板蓝根、艾蒿等天然植物制成的蓝靛溶液。制作时，根据所需花样纹式用线将白布缚着，做成一定襞折的小纹，浸入染缸里浸染。如此反复浸染到一定程度后，取出晾干，拆去缬结，便出现蓝底白花的图案花纹。这些图案多为简单的几何图形，构图严谨，布局丰满，充满生活气息。

Bai Women Making Tie-dyed Fabrics

A traditional art and craft of the Bai people, Tie-dye is a process of dying the white cotton or linen fabrics using indigo dye—usually made of natural plants such as radix isatidis and wormwood from Cangshan Mountain. Major procedures are as follows: fold the white cloth into a pattern, bind it with strings and then dip it into indigo dye. Repeat this process to get the desired effect. After drying out the cloth and removing the strings, blue and white pattern appears. These patterns are mostly simple geometrical figures, feature precise composition and well-rounded layout that present rich flavor of life.

原湖泊，在风平浪静的日子里泛舟洱海，那干净透明的湖面宛如碧澄澄的蓝天，给人以宁静而悠远的感受。

大理国时期这里佛教盛行，家家有佛堂，因此大理国有"佛国"之称。崇圣寺三塔不但是大理的象征，是云南古代历史文化的象征，也是中国南方最古老、最雄伟的建筑群之一。崇圣寺初建于南诏丰祐年间（824—859），现庙宇建筑已毁，只有三塔完好地保留下来。

azalea are grown; when blooming, the flowers are vying with each other in beauty. The spring water, channeled from Cangshan Mountain, flows through every household. Such scenes form the distinctive features of Dali.

Dali sits between Cangshan Mountain and Erhai Lake. Cangshan Mountain, also known as "Diancangshan Mountain", consists of 19 peaks over 3,500 meters above sea level, the highest being over 4,000 meters. Cangshan Mountain enjoys great reputation for its snow, clouds and springs, among

- 大理白族三月街的歌舞表演
  Song and Dance Performances in Sanyue Street, Dali

● 大理苍山

苍山山顶的积雪经夏不消，在风和日丽的阳春三月更显得晶莹娴静，如同水晶世界。

Cangshan Mountain, Dali

The everlasting snow covering the top of Cangshan Mountain sparkles in the sunny spring day; it looks like a crystal world when seen from afar.

崇圣寺三塔由一大二小三座塔组成，大塔叫千寻塔，与南北两个小塔的距离都是70米，呈"三足鼎立"之势。千寻塔高69.13米，为方形密檐式空心砖塔，一共有16级，属于典型的唐代建筑风格。塔身内壁垂直贯通上下，设有木质楼梯，可以登上塔顶。南北两座小塔形制一样，均为10层，高42.4米，为八角形密檐式空心砖塔，外观装饰成阁

which the everlasting snow on Cangshan Mountain ranks first among the four famous scenes (wind, flowers, snow and moon) in Dali. The top of Cangshan Mountain are dotted with many alpine lakes, surrounded by thick primary forests; in between every two peaks are streams, and water rushes down the mountain, adding vitality to the place. Erhai Lake is an alpine lake. On sunny days, it looks just like the sea; boating on the crystal-clear water, one would feel

- **大理崇圣寺三塔**

崇圣寺三塔布局规整，外观协调，大塔显得高大雄伟，又衬托出小塔的玲珑雅致。三塔高耸于蓝天之下，与远处的苍山、洱海相互辉映，成为大理的象征。

The Three Pagodas, Dali

The Three pagodas are well arranged and have balanced and harmonious look. The tall and majestic Qianxun Pagoda brings out the refined elegance of the small ones. Set against the distant backdrop of Cangshan Mountain and Erhai Lake, the towering pagodas became a symbol of culture of Dali.

楼式，塔顶有镏金塔刹宝顶，非常华丽。

大理白族民居以"三坊一照壁""四合五天井"封闭式庭院为典型格局。"三坊一照壁"，即主房一坊，左右厢房二坊，加上主房对面的照壁，合围成一个三合院。

quiet and serene.

Buddhism was very popular in Nanzhao and Dali Period; temples were everywhere, hence Dali was regarded as "Land of Buddha". A symbol of Dali and ancient history and culture in Yunnan, the Three Pagodas of Chongsheng Temple are the oldest and most majestic buildings

"四合五天井"指由正房、下房、左右厢房四坊房屋组成的封闭式四合宅院；除中间一个大天井外，四角还有四个小天井或漏间。三坊一照壁、四合五天井是大理和丽江地区白族民居中最基本、最常见的形式，其他布局形式都是它们的变异、发展和组合。白族民居的山墙一般以白灰粉刷，上用水墨绘以云纹、莲花纹等吉祥图案。

- "三坊一照壁"民居示意图
A Schematic Diagram of "Three Buildings and a Screen Wall"

in southern China. Chongsheng Temple was a Buddhist temple built between 824 and 859; its buildings were destroyed but the three pagodas survived.

The Three Pagodas comprises three independent pagodas forming a symmetric triangle: the biggest one is Qianxun Pagoda, 70 meters apart from the other two. The square-shaped pagoda is of typical architectural style of the Tang Dynasty. It is 69.13 meters in length, and composed of 16 stories, with multiple eaves on each story. The interior of the pagoda is hollow, only a wooden staircase leading to the top. The other two sibling pagodas are of octagonal shape, standing to the north and south of Qianxun Pagoda. Built with bricks, their bodies are hollow, 42.4 meters high in 10 stories. The two loft-style pagodas are surmounted by golden spires, which look majestic and magnificent.

In Dali, houses of the Bai people are usually of closed courtyard style, which is typically divided into two types: (1) "Three buildings and a screen wall". Such house includes a major room, two wing rooms, and a screen wall opposite the principal room. Joined together, they form a closed courtyard. (2) "Courtyard house with five patios". Such compound

和顺

和顺古镇位于腾冲县城西南3公里处，古名"阳温暾"，后因境内有一条小河绕村流过而更名"河顺"，之后又取"士和民顺"之意，定名为"和顺"。明代洪武年间（1368—1398），和顺的先民奉命从四川、南京、湖广等地至此屯垦戍边，世代生息繁衍，距今已有600多年的历史。和顺地处西南古

usually consists of a main building, a front building and wing rooms, adjoined to form a courtyard; in addition to the center patio, there are also four small patios on the four corners. In Dali and Lijiang, these two types of buildings are the most basic forms in Bai dwellings, other forms being developed or altered based upon them. In houses of the Bai people, walls are normally painted white, onto which auspicious patterns such as cloud and lotus are painted in ink.

- 和顺古镇的月台
  Platform, Heshun

丝绸之路的要冲，一代代和顺人为了谋生，顺着古丝道出发，经营贸易，足迹遍布东南亚，和顺由此形成了独特的华侨文化。

和顺四周是大大小小的火山锥，全乡的民居住宅从东到西环山而建，逐渐升高，房舍密集，错落有致。一条三合河绕村而过，两座石拱桥连接村内外的大路。村中所有的道路甚至连村外的田埂都是

Heshun

The old town of Heshun, formerly known as "Yangwendun", sits 3 kilometers southwest of Tengchong County. It was later renamed "Heshun" (smooth river) for the fact that a stream runs round the village. "*He*" (河) that means "river" was later replaced with one of its homonyms "*He*" (和) that means "peace", and the town got its present name. About 600 years ago, in Hongwu Period of the Ming Dynasty, the ancestors

- 弯楼子民居
  Curved Buildings

用石条铺就的，十分整洁。环村的大路与每一条巷道的交会处，都有一道围有石栏的半圆形或扇形"月台"，月台中间种有一棵大榕树或是槐树，绿阴如盖，旁有石凳供人休憩。

和顺镇的"弯楼子"是一组具有当地特色的组合式建筑群，因楼房沿巷道的曲线修砌而得名。这里

• 和顺石板路
Stone-paved Road, Heshun

of Heshun migrated here from Sichuan, Nanjing, Hubei, Hunan and other places at the behest of the emperor, and they lived here generation after generation. Heshun was a communications hub on the ancient Silk Road of southwest China. For hundreds of years, local men were away conducting business far from home, touring extensively all over Southeast Asia. A unique overseas Chinese culture thus formed in Heshun.

Heshun is surrounded by large and small volcanic cones; its dwellings are built embracing the mountain, ascending gradually from east to west following the terrain. When seen from afar, the thickly dotted houses create a well-balanced view. Running round the village is the Sanhe River, over which are two stone arch bridges connecting the main road inside and outside the village. All the roads, including the ridges of field, are stone-paved, appearing trim and neat. In every intersection, where the main road around the village and the alleys meet, there is a semi-circular or fan-shaped platform with stone balustrades; in the center of the platform grows a large banyan tree or a locust tree, under the dense shade of which are stone benches for people to take a rest.

"Curved Buildings" is a group

• 和顺镇河边的洗衣亭

Laundry Pavilion by the Waterside, Heshun

是清道光二十年（1840年）李氏家族创办的跨国商号"永茂和"的旧址，由互相连通的"三坊一照壁"式庭院组成，面积为951平方米，房屋椽梁全用名贵的楸木，历经百年不生蛀虫。宅院布局错落有致，装饰堂皇富丽，属于典型的和顺民居。

在和顺的小河和池塘边，每隔一段距离便会有一个古朴典雅的小亭子，立在水边，村妇可以在小亭子里洗衣。这种独特的洗衣亭，在和顺有六座。洗衣亭可以洗衣、纳凉，也可以遥望远方，寄托相思。和顺男人出走四方，为了让家中女人在洗衣时不被风吹日晒，建了这样的亭子。

of buildings with local features of Heshun, so named because they are built following the curves of the alleys. The buildings were formerly used by "Yongmaohe" — a multinational firm founded by the Li family in 1840. Covering an area of 951 square meters, the complex is of threebuilding-one-screen-wall courtyard style; the rafters and beams in the complex were made of expensive catalpa wood, far from moths and woodworms even after a century. A typical Heshun residence, the complex has a well-arranged layout and magnificent decorations.

At intervals along the rivers or ponds in Heshun, there are simple and elegant pavilions standing by the waterside, where village women do laundry. Heshun boasts six such pavilions. Except for washing clothes and enjoying the cool air, the pavilions were also where the women yearned for their loved ones. Before leaving home for business, the men of Heshun built these pavilions so that their women would not be burned by wind and sun when doing laundry.